COMPUTER SYSTEMS AND COMMUNICATION TECHNOLOGY

Advances in Transdisciplinary Engineering

Transdisciplinary engineering is the exchange of knowledge about product, process, organization, or social environment in the context of innovation. The ATDE book series aims to explore the evolution of engineering, and promote transdisciplinary practices, in which the exchange of different types of knowledge from a diverse range of disciplines is fundamental. The series focuses on international collaboration and providing high-level contributions to the internationally available literature on the theme of the conference.

Volume 49

Recently published in this series

ISSN 2352-751X (print)
ISSN 2352-7528 (online)

Computer Systems and Communication Technology

Proceedings of the 5th International Conference (ICCSCT 2023),
Kuala Lumpur, Malaysia, 24–25 November 2023

Edited by

Wenfeng Zheng

*School of Automation, University of Electronic Science and Technology of
China, Chengdu, Sichuan, China*

IOS Press

Amsterdam • Berlin • Washington, DC

ISBN 978-1-64368-496-3 (print)
ISBN 978-1-64368-497-0 (online)
Library of Congress Control Number: 2024931571
doi: 10.3233/ATDE49

Publisher
IOS Press BV
Nieuwe Hemweg 6B
1013 BG Amsterdam
Netherlands
e-mail: order@iospress.nl

For book sales in the USA and Canada:
IOS Press, Inc.
6751 Tepper Drive
Clifton, VA 20124
USA
Tel.: +1 703 830 6300
Fax: +1 703 830 2300
sales@iospress.com

Preface

We are delighted to present the proceedings of the 2023 5th International Conference on Computer Systems and Communication Technology (ICCSCT 2023), held in Kuala Lumpur, Malaysia, from November 24–25, 2023.

The vision behind ICCSCT 2023 was to establish a premier interdisciplinary platform for researchers, practitioners, and educators to showcase and discuss the latest innovations, trends, challenges, and solutions in the fields of Computer Systems and Engineering, Computer Graphics and Multimedia, and Communication Technology.

The conference comprised three distinct sessions, featuring oral presentations, keynote speeches, and an engaging online Q&A discussion format. With participation from 50 attendees representing 12 countries, including Australia, Canada, China, Germany, India, Kazakhstan, Pakistan, Poland, Nepal, Saudi Arabia, the UK, and the USA, the event showcased a truly global perspective.

A total of 8 keynote speeches and 42 oral presentations enriched the conference agenda. Keynote speakers were allotted 30 minutes each, while oral presenters had 15 minutes, followed by a dynamic 3-minute Question and Answer (Q&A) session.

We extend our heartfelt gratitude to all the authors who submitted papers and the dedicated delegates whose active participation contributed to making ICCSCT a vibrant platform for sharing ideas and innovations.

Special thanks are due to our committee members for their unwavering guidance and support. The commendable efforts of our peer reviewers significantly enhanced the quality of the papers through constructive critical comments, improvements, and corrections. We sincerely appreciate their invaluable contributions, which played a pivotal role in the success of the conference.

Prof. Wenfeng Zheng
Editor of the ICCSCT2023 Proceeding
The University of Electronic Science and Technology of China
Email: winfirms@uestc.edu.cn
https://faculty.uestc.edu.cn/zhengwenfeng/en/index.htm

About the Conference

Peer Review Statement
Submitted papers: 66
Accepted peer reviewed papers: 10

Peer Reviewers
Tilemachos Koliopoulos, University of West Attica
Jonayet Miah, University of South Dakota
Mamadou Diahame, Ecole Supérieur Polytechnique de Dakar
Konstantin Ryabinin, Perm State National Research University
Anwer Ghedamsi, Université de Tunis
Moazzam Nazir, Clemson University
Mamady Delamou, Mohammed Vi Polytechnic University
Xavier Vilanova, Universitat Rovira i Virgili
Rajesh Kumar, Division of Instrumentation and Control Engineering, Netaji Subhas
    Institute of Technology
Tung Lam Nguyen, Hawaii Natural Energy Institute
Vipasha Sharma, Department of Computer Science & Engineering, Chandigarh
    University
Ivan Diryana Sudirman, Binus Business School
Xing Xu, Jiangsu University
Hui Lin, Shenyang Ligong University
Yadong Liu, Shanghai Jiao Tong University
Ling Guo Liu, Northeast Electric Power University
Ming Xu, Shenzhen University
Shengxin Lin, China University of Mining and Technology
Rui Zhang, Kunming University of Science and Technology
Shengxin Lin, China University of Mining and Technology

Conference Organization

General Chair
Prof. Wenfeng Zheng, University of Electronic Science and Technology of China

General Co-Chair
Prof. Fairouz Kamareddine, Heriot-Watt University, Edinburgh, Scotland

Program Committee Chair
Prof. Yaohui Li, Xuchang University, China

Technical Program Chairs
Assoc. Prof. Ka-Chun Wong, City University of Hong Kong, China
Assoc. Prof. Pavel Loskot, Zhejiang University | Zju-Uiuc Institute, China

Technical Program Committee
Prof. Schahram Dustdar, Distributed Systems Group (DSG), TU Wien, Austria
Prof. Dr. Rui Ming Fang, Huaqiao University, China
Prof. Phalguni Gupta, NITTTR, Kolkata, India
Assoc. Prof. Yaohui Li, Xuchang University, China
Prof. Dr. Abdel-Badeeh M. Salem, Ain Shams University, Cairo, Egypt
Prof. Dr. Lu Lu, School of Computer Science & Engineering, South China University
    of Technology, China
Asst. Prof. Nahid Farhady Ghalaty, Texas Tech University, TX, USA
Asst. Prof. Cui Liang, Chong Qing University, China
Prof. Dr. Kuma Kida, Toyo University, Japan
Dr. Youn Kim Jee, Kyung Hee University, Korea
Dr. Xiaoping Zhou, Beijing University of Civil Engineering and Architecture, China
Assoc. Prof. Ming Li, School of Electrical Engineering and Intelligentization,
    Dongguan University of Technology, China
Prof. Jain-shing Liu, Providence University, Taiwan
Asst. Prof. Sook Ha, Virginia Military Institute, USA
Prof. Ka Lok Man, Xi'an Jiaotong-Liverpool University, China
Prof. Dr. Ismail Rakip Karas, Karabük University, Turkey
Prof. Juntao Fei, Hohai University, China
Prof. Chao-Tung Yang, Tunghai University, Taiwan
Prof. Zhiyuan Shen, Nanjing University of Aeronautics and Astronautics, China
Dr. Yuan Ren LOKE, Nanyang Technological University, Singapore
Dr. Natarajan Meghanathan, Jackson State University, USA
Dr. Hossam Kasem, Shenzhen University, China
Prof. Xiaokun Yang, University of Houston, Clear Lake, USA
Prof. Zoran Gajic, Rutgers University, USA
Prof. Shadi Abudalfa, King Fahd University of Petroleum and Minerals, Saudi Arabia
Prof. José Santa Lozano, Polytechnic University of Cartagena, Spain
Dr. Abdul Ghani Albaali, Princess Sumaya University, Jordan
Dr. Alex Roney Mathew, Bethany College, West Virginia, USA
Dr. Paul Craig, Xi'an Jiaotong-Liverpool University, China
Assoc. Prof. Bahman Javadi, Western Sydney University, Australia
Prof. Raja Kumar Murugesan, Taylor's University, Malaysia
Prof. Amin Beheshti, Macquarie University, Australia
Prof. Yu-Chen Hu, Providence University, Taiwan
Dr. Shekhar R, Alliance University, India
Prof. Beligiannnis Grigorios, University of Patras, Greece
Assoc. Prof. Xiaojian Liu, Xi'an University of Science and Technology, China
Prof. ZhaoYang Dong, The University of New South Wales, Australia
Dr. Md. Kafiul Islam, Independent University, Bangladesh
Dr. Xujuan Zhou, University of the Southern Queensland, Australia
Dr. Xinggang Yan, University of Kent, UK
Prof. Karl Christoph Ruland, University of Siegen, Germany
Prof. Jyotsna Kumar Mandal, University of Kalyani, India
Prof. Yassine Salih-Alj, Al Akhawayn University
Asst. Prof. Cong Pu, Marshall University, USA
Prof. Bin Fu, University of Texas Rio Grande Valley, USA
Prof. James C.N. Yang, National Dong Hwa University, Taiwan

Contents

Computer Systems and Communication Technology
W. Zheng (Ed.)
doi:10.3233/ATDE240002

1

Application Research of Computer Statistics System in the Construction of Public Sports Service System for National Fitness in Free Trade Port

Weiguo Chen[a], Qiuxiang Xie[b1], Qinqin Yang[c], Yanlong Hao[d], Wenting Hao[e]

[a]*Hainan College of Vocation and Technique, Haikou, 571100, China*
[b]*Haikou University of Economics, Haikou, 572022, China*
[c]*Xinjiang Police Academy, Urumqi, 830011, China*
[d]*University of Sanya, Sanya, 572022, China*
[e]*Hainan Vocational and Technical College of Economy and Trade, Haikou, 571127, China*

Abstract: The reconstruction of public sports service system is the core issue facing the construction of free trade port. Through the investigation of the status quo of public sports service system in the construction of free trade port, the gap between Hainan free trade port and international and domestic public sports service system is concluded through computer statistical analysis and research. And then through the expert demonstration, under the leadership and support of the government, a series of public sports service system and industrial development policies and measures suitable for the construction of free trade ports are formulated.

Keywords: Computer statistical system, public sports service system, free trade port, sports industry

1. Research on public sports service system at home and abroad

1.1. Research status of foreign public sports service system

In the western developed countries with capital market economy, sports has long become an industrial sector, especially since the 1970s, with the economic development of various countries, the scale of sports industry has gradually expanded, the economic function of sports has been continuously developed, and the sports industry has shown a rapid and international development trend. The sports industry has become an important industry in the national economy in many countries, and some have even become pillar industries, such as the United States, Italy, the United Kingdom and other developed countries. Other developed countries such as France, Germany, Japan and other countries also have a considerable scale of sports industry.

---

[1] Corresponding Author: Qiuxiang Xie, 13006025126@163.com

Since the 1990s, due to the increasingly obvious role of sports in promoting the economy, some developed countries have put forward the concept of "total national sports output value". And the sports industry policy has been formulated, and the sports industry has become a veritable important economic sector in the developed countries, and occupies an important position in the national economic system.

In terms of the specific sports management system, Japan and South Korea carry out the typical sports management system of government management; England, Australia, New Zealand, Spain and Singapore adopt integrated sports management system. The United States, Italy, Germany, Sweden and Norway adopt the sports management system of community management.

1.2. Research status of domestic public sports service system

Under the condition of socialist planned economy, sports undertakings in our country adopt the mode of running sports by the whole people, and completely rely on the financial allocation and investment of the state. The relationship between sports and economy is expressed as the relationship between sports and finance, and sports is a pure consumption sector. The amount of national financial investment in sports not only affects the speed and structure of sports development and growth, but also indirectly determines the influence of sports growth on economic growth [1].

With the establishment of the socialist market economy, China's economic base and social environment have undergone significant changes. At present, the process of sports industrialization in China is in a shallow management stage. As an economic sector [2], sports is not mature in scale, structure and level, and its economic function is far from being developed. In recent years, the State General Administration of Sport, the National Development and Reform Commission and the Ministry of Finance have worked out a number of policy opinions on promoting the development of the sports industry through a large number of investigations and studies, and gradually improve the situation. But generally speaking, the public sports service system in our country is not perfect[3], the sports industry level and the sports industrial policy are not commensurate with the national conditions.

The construction of Hainan International Tourism Island has been approved for a short period of time, which is suitable for Hainan's public sports service system and sports construction industrial policy, and in-depth research has not been carried out, especially in county-level cities, there are few large sports buildings, and the public sports service system is not sound enough. The picture below is a comprehensive sports stadium in a village in Hainan Island (see the picture below)[4]. Under the background of the construction of international tourism island, the research of Hainan's public sports service system and sports industry policy is basically a blank in terms of content and perspective.

2. Research purpose

The construction of Hainan Free Trade Port has been included in the overall national development plan. Through the investigation, computer statistics, analysis and research on the status quo of public sports service system, sports buildings and industries in the construction of free trade port[5], the gap between the development of public sports service system, sports buildings and industries in Hainan free trade Port and the international and domestic sports construction industries is concluded. And then through the expert argumentation, with the support of the government, formulate a series of sports construction industrial policies suitable for the construction of free trade ports. It mainly includes: Hainan Province sports finance and financing policy, Hainan Province sports tax policy, Hainan Province sports tourism policy, Hainan Province sports competition management policy, Hainan Province sports laws, regulations, policies and so on. Put forward the free trade port public sports service system, sports building and industry construction planning, to make positive contributions to the construction of Hainan free trade port[6].

Figure 1. A multi-sport complex in a village on Hainan Island

2.1. Implement the basic state policy of building free trade ports

1.Several Opinions on Promoting the Construction and Development of Hainan Free Trade Port issued by The State Council

Article 12 of The State Council's "Several Opinions on Promoting the Construction and Development of Free Trade Ports" clearly proposes to "accelerate the development of culture, sports and exhibition industries"[7], and for the first time proposes to "pilot some internationally accepted tourism, sports and entertainment projects in Hainan, and explore the development of guessing sports lottery and large-scale international events." It can be seen that the sports industry is an important link in the construction of Hainan international tourism island, and the formulation of corresponding sports industry policies has become the top priority in the construction of international tourism island.

2.The CPC Hainan Provincial Committee and the People's Government of Hainan Province shall implement the decision of The State Council on Several Opinions on Promoting the Construction and Development of Hainan International Tourism Island

In the "Decision", Hainan Province focuses on the development of the sports industry among the ten major events: First, the transformation and upgrading of Hainan Happy Festival, planning and organizing a number of influential cultural entertainment, festivals, exhibitions and sports events, and striving to achieve a festival month by month. The second is to set up a tourism development investment and financing platform, make good use of the special subsidy funds given by the central finance to the construction of Hainan International Tourism Island, and strive to make it an incubator of key tourism development projects in the province. This provides a starting point for the formulation of Hainan sports industry policy from two aspects: funds and event management.

3. Hainan Province "Hainan International Tourism Island Construction and Development Plan Outline"

In the outline of the Plan for the construction and development of Hainan International Tourism Island (2010-2020), it is clearly proposed to vigorously develop the cultural and sports industry, especially the sports and fitness industry. Actively develop the sports and fitness industry, hold sports events with Hainan characteristics, and cultivate the sports and fitness market. We will vigorously develop coastal sports such as diving, sailing, windsurfing, surfing, fishing, beach volleyball, beach football, and outdoor sports such as cycling, mountaineering, rafting, and field development. At the same time, it puts forward investment and financing policies and fiscal and tax policies in terms of policy measures, which points out the direction for Hainan sports industry policy research[8].

4. Hainan Provincial People's Government "Hainan International Tourism Island Construction Action Plan"

According to the Action Plan for the Construction of Hainan International Tourism Island, there are three basic connotations of the construction of Hainan International Tourism Island: establishing new goals, establishing new systems, and implementing new policies. The most prominent one is "new". At present, the main work of fully launching the construction of Hainan international tourism island includes building an international tourism service guarantee system. Sports tourism is an important part of Hainan tourism, which provides the necessity and feasibility for the research of sports building policy under the background of Hainan Free Trade Port.

2.2. Provide policy support for the construction of public sports service system and the development of sports buildings in the free trade port

At present, the sports buildings in Hainan are mainly some "extensive construction" of lower grade and more obsolete. Compared with the large sports buildings in Beijing, Shanghai and Guangzhou in China, the development of sports buildings appears to be inadequate. There are many restricting factors, but the lack and imperfection of sports building policy cannot be ignored. Without the formulation and improvement of sports industry policy, the development of Hainan sports industry will lose its vitality. This study is expected to help the development of public sports service system in Hainan Free Trade Port in the following aspects, and inject vitality into the development of Hainan sports industry.

1. In terms of public sports service system and general policies of sports industry, sports asset management and development policies, sports investment policies, sports market management policies, sports tax policies, sports labor service price policies, etc., can be applied to all aspects of investment, operation and management of sports industry policies.

2. In terms of sports main industrial policies, the formulation of competitive sports industrial policies, mass sports industrial policies, sports venues industrial policies, sports education and technology industrial policies, sports intangible assets

development and management policies, sports lottery management policies, etc., can promote the initial formation of the sports industry system.

3. In terms of sports-related industrial policies, mature sports industrial policies can clarify the connotation and extension of sports-related industries, which is conducive to the relevant departments to jointly hold sports commodity fairs and exhibitions on a regular basis, activate the sports economy, and promote sports commodity exchanges. From the perspective of sports, we guide, consult, help, inspect and supervise the production and operation of various sports-related products, and adopt various ways, methods and means to continuously expand and improve the variety of sports products[9].

4. In terms of sports internal industrial policy, a sound sports industrial policy can clarify the property rights relationship, reasonably evaluate and protect state-owned assets, on the one hand, strictly prevent the loss in various ways, on the other hand, ensure the due income; Government and enterprise enterprises should be strictly separated, independent accounting, and the content of the body-run industry should gradually be as close as possible to sports and transform to the main industry of sports.

3. Research method

3.1. Research object

*Investment, manag*ement and operation of Hainan's public sports service system and sports (social sports, competitive sports) industry under the background of international free trade port construction[10].

3.2. Research steps and processes

1. Consult and collect domestic and foreign literature on sports industry policy research by the literature data method; Determine the research direction, apply for the project, and lay a good foundation for further research.

2. On the basis of existing literature, the Questionnaire on the Status quo of Sports Industry in International Tourism Island was prepared by expert investigation method and expert opinions were solicited, and the reliability and validity were tested. 1000 copies of the questionnaire were printed. Conduct a comprehensive survey on Hainan sports industry and obtain relevant data.

3. Use computer technology, U inspection and comparative analysis methods to organize, statistical analysis and inference of survey data and information (see the following (1) (2)), and obtain the feasibility of the development of the public sports service system and the sports industry in international tourism islands. Sexual conclusion. At the same time, according to the actual situation of the construction of international tourism islands, the relevant experts formulate various sports industry policies in Hainan.

$$u = \frac{(\bar{X}_1 - \bar{X}_2) - (\mu_1 - \mu_2)}{S_{\bar{X}_1 - \bar{X}_2}} (\sim N(0,1))$$

(1)

$$u = \frac{\bar{X}_1 - \bar{X}_2}{\sqrt{\dfrac{S_1^2}{n_1} + \dfrac{S_2^2}{n_2}}}$$

(2)

4. Submit the preliminary development of various international tourism island sports industry policies to relevant experts and government departments, solicit guidance and suggestions, and obtain corresponding support.

5. According to the feedback of experts and leaders, the project team will be organized again to conduct statistical analysis and discussion on the data, and form "Sports Industry Policy of International Tourism Island", "Research and Experiment Report on Sports industry Policy of International Tourism Island" and relevant papers.

6. Organize 5 experts in sports, law and economics to discuss the first draft of the "Free Trade Port Sports Industry Policy Research and Experiment Report" and related papers, and put forward suggestions for improvement.

7. Writing and revising project papers and concluding research reports.

4. Conclusion and suggestion

Through the statistical analysis and research of the data obtained from the inspection and investigation, the gap between Hainan sports industry and the international and domestic sports buildings and the industrial developed cities is concluded. After expert argumentation, the following conclusions are drawn.

1）In the construction of the free trade port, the effective use of non-public capital, especially international capital, can help promote the development of Hainan's public sports service system and sports construction industry, and broaden the funding channels for the construction of the free trade port.

2） Sports tourism is the living soul in the construction of an international tourism island, and sports tourism will soon become the mainstay of Hainan's tourism market. At the same time, it is also a powerful driving force for the development of public sports services and sports industry in Hainan.

3） Reasonable sports tax policies can effectively regulate the development of sports construction industry in Hainan. It is necessary to further explore the characteristics of the tax policy of Hainan sports industry under the construction of free trade port.

4） In the construction of free trade ports, the development prospects of mass sports industry are broad. We will improve mass sports organizations, improve the public sports service system for national fitness, and provide more and better sports public services for domestic and foreign tourists and Hainan people.

5） Sports lottery is the driving force for the development of sports construction industry, and further improve the issuance and management of sports lottery. The sports lottery has become an inexhaustible driving force for the development of Hainan sports construction industry.

6）Interaction and common development between sports teaching, scientific research, public sports service system and sports construction industrial policy. The cultivation of professional sports talents is conducive to the implementation and development of sports construction industry policy.

7）In the context of free trade port construction, Hainan should continue to promote the reform and innovation of sports buildings. To adapt to the new situation of the continuous development of the socialist market economy, we should constantly innovate the development system of sports construction with the spirit of reform and innovation, and promote the coordinated development of sports construction industry in Hainan.

Acknowledgements:

Hainan Province Philosophy and Social Science planning project "Sports + Tourism to help the coordinated development of Hainan Beautiful rural Sports Culture" project number: HNSK(YB)23-53

About author: Chen Weiguo, 1979.02, male, Han nationality, Qionghai, Hainan, lecturer, research interests: University physical education and social sports research.

Corresponding author: Xie Qiuxiang, 1987.04, female, Han nationality, Lecturer, Haikou University of Economics, research direction: Physical education and college students' mental health education

References

[1]   Several Opinions of The State Council on Promoting the Construction and Development of Hainan International Tourism Island, Guofa (2009) No. 44
[2]   Hainan Provincial People's Government "Hainan International Tourism Island Construction and Development Plan Outline (2010-2020)
[3]   Speech by Liu Peng, Director of the General Administration of Sport of China and Wang Jun, Deputy Director of the General Administration of Sport, at the 2005 National Sports Industry Work Conference [Z].
[4]   Liu DL: Sports Industry Management and Management Knowledge [M] Beijing: China Labor and Social Security Press,2005.6 First edition
[5]   Qiu XD. How to Develop Sports Gambling Industry as soon as possible after China's entry into WTO [J] Journal of Beijing Sport University, 2003,(06)
[6]   Chen BZ: Research on the development and Countermeasures of Sports Tourism in China [J] Journal of Beijing Sport University,2007 (1)
[7]   Hao WT, Concise Statistical Methods of Sports, Xinjiang University Press, August 1996.
[8]   Liu H, Hao WT, Sports Measurement and Evaluation, Guangxi Normal University Press, August 2005.
[9]   Li XR, "Research on the Status Quo and Countermeasures of the Implementation of National Fitness Project in Urban Communities in China" [J] Sports Science, 02, 2001.
[10]   Wang Y, Zhou CH, Research on the Implementation of Sports Industry Policy in Hunan Province at the present stage [J] Journal of Capital Institute of Physical Education, 4th issue, 2009.

Computer Systems and Communication Technology
W. Zheng (Ed.)
© *2024 The Authors.*
This article is published online with Open Access by IOS Press and distributed under the terms
of the Creative Commons Attribution Non-Commercial License 4.0 (CC BY-NC 4.0).
doi:10.3233/ATDE240003

Improving Mass Gathering Management Using Process Mining Techniques

Amirah ALHARBI[1]
Computer Science and Artificial Intelligence department
Computing College
Umm Al-Qura University
Kingdom of Saudi Arabia
ORCID ID: https://orcid.org/0000-0002-7449-0642

Abstract. Crowd management is a significant topic especially for countries that support gathering events frequently. The Kingdom of Saudi Arabia hosts and manages one of the world class annual religious gatherings known as "pilgrimage". Several challenges are raised for managing and controlling such mass gathering event. In this paper we propose a comprehensive framework for event processes modelling and management. The framework consists of four main stages starts with acquiring temporal data and ends by modelling different processes of the event. The main contribution of this work is to demonstrate how process mining techniques can be used innovatively to model the movement flow of crowd. Synthetic data is used to show a proof-of-concept of the proposed framework and the applicability of using it in modelling and monitoring real crowd movement scenarios.

Keywords. Process mining, crowd management, modelling, pattern discovery

1. Introduction

Every year, millions of pilgrims from different countries and backgrounds participate in this event, creating a massive crowd. The term crowd in most literature is referred to a group of people without strict quantification as mentioned in the research [1] . However, crowd density aims to estimate the number of people in square meter [2] . There is different understanding of the term crowd management, the most relevant definition for pilgrimage which known as "Hajj" context can be thought as utilizing path analysis and theories of decision-making enables the creation of models that depict how crowds behave in different situations includes emergencies. From this perspective, these models minimize assumptions about individual behaviors and concentrate more on grasping the mainstream dynamics of the crowd. On the other hand, crowd management can be defined as control strategies involving a cooperative endeavor among various members of the crowd management team and the crowd itself [3]. The effectiveness of these strategies relies on the efficient collection, distribution, and communication of information. The well-being and satisfaction of the crowd depends on the accomplishments of these joint initiatives. Most of the research that discussed crowd issue has focused on one of three aspects which are crowd modelling,

---

[1] Corresponding Author: Amirah Alharbi, email: amnharbi@uqu.edu.sa

crowd monitoring and crowd management. Crowd modelling focuses on the use of various simulation tools as discussed elaborately in the survey [4] while crowd monitoring mainly relies on computer vision approaches as presented in [5]. Both of crowd modelling and crowd monitoring research has goal which is providing better crowd management.

Understanding the problem specifications is critical for developing robust Hajj crowd management tool. Start to End Hajj journey consists of several phases.

An abstraction of the process and its structure is demonstrated in Figure 1 below. Every phase of Hajj journey consists of different processes and every process contains at least one activity. Transition from one activity to another represented by physical movements between different positions using different public transportations such as buses and trams or on foot (which is the most popular way for young pilgrims).

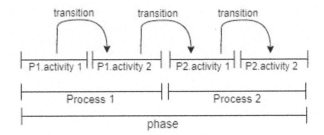

Figure 1. Components of phase

The aim of this paper is to build a crowed movement modelling and monitoring system using temporal and spatial data of Hajj journey at the holy sites in Saudi Arabia. The technique of process mining can be used as a novel approach in this research. Process mining [7] is a type of data mining that mainly uses event logs (which store time, event, unique ID for every single action taken in a system) to generate process model and show what has happened in reality. Also, the temporal data can be used to classify different types of Hajj experiences represented in trajectory forms based on some demographics data, for example, age, educational level or country of origin. The main objectives of this work include the following:

1. Providing a real-time streaming for pilgrims' movement on both individual and groups-campaign level at the holy sites locations.

2. Implementing an alert-based tool to predict possible lost pilgrims based on their movement route where pilgrim is supposed to be in a predefined location based on their campaign zone or other expected locations related to rituals activities.

3. Developing a precaution detection tool of unusual crowd movement.

This paper is divided into two parts, the first part explores different techniques that can be used to monitor and track target objects. In the second part we present the main contribution of this work by demonstrating how temporal data can be used to model the flow of movement.

2. Related work

One of the most significant challenges discussed in [8] is ensuring the safety and security of the pilgrims. The sheer number of people in one place can lead to overcrowding and stampedes, which have unfortunately resulted in numerous fatalities in the past.

Additionally, the logistics of accommodating such many people, including transportation, lodging, and food, is a significant challenge [9]. The gathering of millions of people in a confined space for an extended period can create challenges in maintaining public health and providing medical services. Some of the healthcare issues that arise during Hajj include disease transmission. The proximity of pilgrims from different regions increases the risk of infectious disease transmission as mentioned in [10].

Finally, Hajj attracts Muslims from all around the world, bringing together diverse cultures, languages, and customs. Some of the challenges arising from cultural differences such as language barriers where pilgrims coming from various countries, communication can be a significant hurdle [11].

Different languages and dialects can hinder effective communication between pilgrims and with the local population, including healthcare providers and authorities. Furthermore, each culture may have its own customs and practices related to religious rituals and behavior. These variations can lead to misunderstandings or conflicts between pilgrims from different cultural backgrounds, requiring additional efforts to promote understanding and tolerance. Moreover, mass gathering events such as Hajj event has a restricted spatial area that may pose a challenge of finding the optimal distributing of facilities and services, for example healthcare center [12].

2.1. The Significance of Process Modelling in Streamlining the Hajj Pilgrimage Experience

The novelty of this work is presented in showing how process mining techniques can be used in modelling Hajj ritual processes. The literature has plenty of research that tried to model Hajj process however, most of them rely on simulation techniques as discussed by [4]. The work presented in [6] discussed an agent-based methodology to simulate the process of Tawaf and stoning the pillars in order to curb the spread of COVID-19.

It should be noted that this research aims to model the full trajectories of Hajj rituals in the holy sites. For this objective, process modeling can be a valuable tool in streamlining the Hajj pilgrimage experience. By mapping out the various steps involved in the process, local movement in Mina, moving toward stoning the pillars and exit from it, going to train stations and then to the Holy Mosque.

Additionally, process modeling can help identify potential bottlenecks and enable planners to take action to mitigate them. By streamlining the process and reducing wait times, pilgrims can have a more enjoyable and stress-free experience.

2.2. Process Mining

Process mining [7] is becoming popular in recent research and can be considered as a type of data mining with focus on temporal data. Any information system has an event log that records every event (action) occurred within the system. Hence, process mining aims to discover start-end process that shows how different events constitute the full process. This relatively new technology plays a significant role in improving the process, with solutions such as real-time data analysis, crowd monitoring, and bottleneck discovery to provide insightful information and assist to monitor the trajectories of crowd (pilgrims) movement. There are three main goals of process mining techniques which are process discovery, conformance checking and then process enhancement [7]. Process discovery algorithms take event log and then build process model based on the events recorded on that log. Conformance checking algorithms measure the compatibility between process model and logs while process enhancement can be achieved by analyzing the process model and identifying some improvements areas [17].

2.2.1. Components of Process Mining

The cornerstone of process mining is event log which must include three types of data; unique ID, event name and timestamp showing when this event occurred. In the context of Hajj, the event name may represent the name of predefined key locations that exist on the holy sites map such as: camps coordinate, Jamarat bridge, train stations and other services. On the other hand, the timestamp is the time the pilgrimage is observed on that location. The third element is the unique ID which corresponds to any E-wristbands that are provided for pilgrims or in this paper, face-id.

2.2.2. Process Mining Tools and Techniques

There are many tools for process mining projects and the most prominent tool for researchers is ProM [18] (Process Mining) in addition to some commercial tools for example, Disco (Discovery) [19], Celonis [20]. Other process mining packages are available on Rstudio and Python.
    The main algorithms can be used in process discovery are:
- Heuristic Miner [21] is developed to address issues of noise and gaps within event logs, its primary focus is on unveiling connections between events – for instance, uncovering the interdependence between two events. The method of creating a process model using a Heuristic Miner is outlined through three steps. The initial step entails extracting information about dependencies and event frequencies.The subsequent step involves constructing a graph based on this dependency and frequency data. The final step involves crafting a process model based on the insights from the second step.
- Fuzzy Miner [22], which revolves around streamlining process models generated within highly adaptable settings, such as hospital environments. Using a straightforward mechanism, the fuzzy miner aims to identify events of high frequency and retain them. Events that occur less frequently but hold substantial connections are grouped into clusters, whereas events with lower frequency and fewer connections are eliminated.
- Inductive Miner [23] is aimed to investigate processes by accommodating various process model configurations. Its development was driven by the need to address model unsoundness, a significant constraint encountered in the Heuristic Miner. This tool employs a divide and conquer strategy, recursively segmenting the log into sub-logs.

3. Method

In this paper, we intend to explore the potential of using temporal and spatial data to optimize the Hajj pilgrimage process through process mining techniques. The proposed methodology has four steps as shown in Figure 2 which are:

Step1: Acquiring temporal/spatial data

Identifying sources of temporal/spatial data is a critical step in our methodology. There are many approaches suggested to collect this kind of data, however, the approach [24] is promising since it is tested on crowd place and does not require a wearable device or smart phone to capture the time-coordinate for people.

Step2: Constructing complete event log

An event log should be in the form of row-based data where every row represents a single event with its related attributes, for example time and position.

Step3: Building process model using process mining tools

Applying process mining discovery techniques to build the model. In this step a process mining tool should be selected in order to investigate various discovery algorithms to build the model. It should be noted that each process discovery algorithm can generate a different model depending on the strategy that is used in the algorithm. Some algorithms focus on determining concurrent events and some of them are designed to cope with the complexity (variability) of the process.

Step4: Visualize and analyze the model

The generated process model from step 3 can be visualized and animated to demonstrate the real flow of the process. This is the most significant advantage of a process model where it shows the actual flow that has happened unlike other simulation tools that just illustrate the flow of what-if questions for scenarios that might happen.

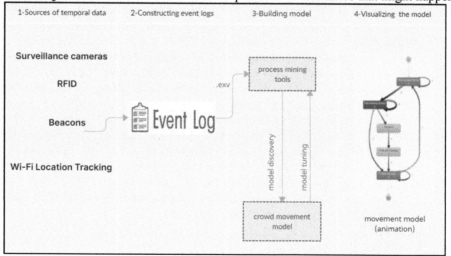

Figure 2. A comprehensive methodology for discovering and monitoring the pilgrimage process.

The generated model can be linked to the current operational dashboard that is used in the holy sites administration center. It is worthy to mention that the proposed dashboard system can be built to demonstrate Hajj process model of different levels for example, movement inside zones or campaign location and cross holy sites.

4. Experiment

To validate the proposed methodology this experiment is conducted over a small spatial process that can happen in Mina for the 10th, 11th, 12th of Hajj days. In this experiment, we want to model the ritual process of stoning the pillars that includes the movement between the camping zones and stoning bridge.

Due to the restrictions of Data Subject Access Request (DSAR) with the authorized party of getting the data a synthetic event log is used here. The fictional data generated from an event log generator which is Gena [28]. This log generator is implemented as plugin in ProM6 Process Mining tool (open source).

Table 1. sample of synthetic event log of Mina events

Id	Location of interest	Time	Normal/Abnormal
5a0be9e0-1b15	camp1	2023-07-27 9:10:00	normal
5c0242ac12147	camp2	2023-07-27 9:13:00	normal
be56-0242ac12	camp2	2023-07-27 8:55:00	normal
be56-0242ac76	camp3	2023-07-27 9:20:00	normal
be56-0242ac3e	camp3	2023-07-27 9:10:00	normal
5a00242ac12h	service center 1	2023-07-27 9:10:45	normal
5a0bf570-024	stoning bridge	2023-07-27 9:39:00	normal
5a0bf69c-1b1	stoning bridge	2023-07-27 9:1:00	normal
5a0bf69c-1b1	Mina Border	2023-07-27 11:51:00	abnormal
5a0bf7c8-1b8	train station	2023-07-27 9:50:00	normal
5a0bf8fe-1bu3	train station	2023-07-27 9:5550	normal
5a0bfa16-1b9	train station	2023-07-27 9:55:08	normal

5. Results and Discussion

Feeding the event log (sample in Table 1) into the ProM6 tool has generated the process model presented in Figure3. The technique of Fuzzy miner algorithm is used to discover the process model. As can be seen from Figure3 there are 9 locations and the links between these locations correspond to the pilgrim's movement. The model shows there is congestion between 'Stoning Bridge' and the local train station which requires more attention to be paid to provide alternatives methods for transferring pilgrims to the holy mosque. Also, the model captures the time when pilgrims located in camp 3 started moving to do pillar stoning ritual event. Interestingly, using this approach of process mining has detected an outlier movement for pilgrims who are headed outside Mina boundaries.

The findings here are restricted to the input event log for proof-of-concept purposes therefore; richer and actual logs will give useful insights.

The benefits of implementing a comprehensive framework for Hajj process management are numerous. Improved crowd management and safety measures can prevent incidents and save lives. Streamlining the process and reducing wait times can improve the overall experience for pilgrims, leading to increased satisfaction and a more positive perception of the event. Additionally, a comprehensive framework can help ensure a coordinated effort and effective implementation of measures, leading to greater efficiency and cost savings.

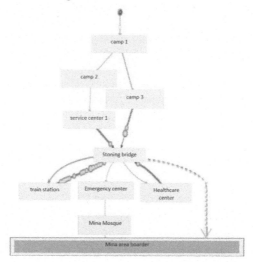

Figure 3. Partial Hajj process model

Implementing a comprehensive framework for Hajj process management can be challenging, as it involves a coordinated effort from various stakeholders with differing priorities and agendas. Additionally, there may be resistance to change from those who are accustomed to the current system. Finally, there may be logistical challenges in implementing new technology and other solutions, such as infrastructure requirements and training needs. It is essential to customize the framework for Hajj process management to cater to the unique needs of different groups of pilgrims. For example, elderly or disabled pilgrims may require special accommodations or assistance, while families with young children may have different needs than single travelers. By taking these factors into account, planners can ensure that all pilgrims have a positive and meaningful experience.

With the number of pilgrims to the Hajj increasing each year, it is essential to scale up the framework for Hajj process management to accommodate this growth. This may involve expanding infrastructure, increasing staffing levels, and implementing new technology and other solutions to improve efficiency and streamline the process. The key success factors in implementing the framework for Hajj process management include stakeholder collaboration, effective communication, and a focus on the needs and comfort of the pilgrims. Additionally, a commitment to continuous improvement and evaluation can help ensure that the framework remains effective and relevant over time.

Acknowledgment

The author would like to thank the Deanship of Scientific Research at Umm Al-Qura University for supporting this work by Grant Code: (23UQU43101400DSR001)

References

[1]   M. S. Zitouni, H. Bhaskar, J. Dias, and M. E. Al-Mualla, "Advances and trends in visual crowd analysis: A systematic survey and evaluation of crowd modelling techniques," *Neurocomputing*, vol. 186, pp. 139–159, Apr. 2016, doi: 10.1016/j.neucom.2015.12.070.

[2]   G. K. Still, *Applied crowd science*. CRC Press, 2021, https://doi.org/10.1201/9781351053068

[3]   C. Martella, J. Li, C. Conrado, and A. Vermeeren, "On current crowd management practices and the need for increased situation awareness, prediction, and intervention," *Saf Sci*, vol. 91, pp. 381–393, Jan. 2017, doi: 10.1016/j.ssci.2016.09.006.

[4]   A. Owaidah, D. Olaru, M. Bennamoun, F.-D. Sohel, and N. Khan, "Review of Modelling and Simulating Crowds at Mass Gathering Events: Hajj as a Case Study," 2019, 10.18564/jasss.3997

[5]   U. Singh, J. F. Determe, F. Horlin, and P. De Doncker, "Crowd Monitoring: State-of-the-Art and Future Directions," *IETE Technical Review (Institution of Electronics and Telecommunication Engineers, India)*, vol. 38, no. 6. Taylor and Francis Ltd., pp. 578–594, 2021. doi: 10.1080/02564602.2020.1803152.

[6]   S. M. Alshammari, M. H. Ba-Aoum, N. A. Alganmi, and A. A. Allinjawi, "Agent-based simulation framework for epidemic forecasting during hajj seasons in Saudi Arabia," *Information (Switzerland)*, vol. 12, no. 8, Aug. 2021, doi: 10.3390/info12080325.

[7]   W. M. P. van der Aalst, *Process Mining: Data Science in Action*. Springer Berlin Heidelberg, 2016. [Online]. Available: https://books.google.co.uk/books?id=hUEGDAAAQBAJ

[8]   E. A. Felemban et al., "Digital revolution for Hajj crowd management: a technology survey," *IEEE Access*, vol. 8, pp. 208583–208609, 2020, doi: 10.1109/ACCESS.2020.3037396.

[9]   E. A. Felemban, "Towards Building an Interactive Platform for Analyzing Movement of Buses in Hajj," *2019 IEEE International Conference on Big Data (Big Data)*, 2019, doi: 10.1109/BigData47090.2019.9005521.

[10] S. Benkouiten, J. A. Al-Tawfiq, Z. A. Memish, A. Albarrak, and P. Gautret, "Clinical respiratory infections and pneumonia during the Hajj pilgrimage: A systematic review," *Travel Med Infect Dis*, vol. 28, pp. 15–26, 2019, DOI: 10.1016/j.tmaid.2018.12.002

[11] H. Majid, "HAJJRAH: An innovative application for pilgrims of Hajj and Umrah," *ARPN journal of engineering and applied sciences*, 2016,doi: 5891308da6fdc

[12] M. Alotaibi, G. Clarke, and N. Malleson, "Optimal service planning in a temporary city," *Journal of Service Science and Management*, vol. 13, no. 05, p. 709, 2020, DOI: 10.4236/jssm.2020.135045

[13] M. M. Almutairi, D. Apostolopoulou, G. Halikias, A. A. Abi Sen, and M. Yamin, "A Framework for Comprehensive Crowd and Hajj Management," in *2022 9th International Conference on Computing for Sustainable Global Development (INDIACom)*, IEEE, 2022, pp. 63–68, doi: 10.23919/INDIACom54597.2022.9763174.

[14] M. Yamin, A. M. Basahel, and A. A. Abi Sen, "Managing crowds with wireless and mobile technologies," *Wirel Commun Mob Comput*, vol. 2018, 2018, https://doi.org/10.1155/2018/7361597

[15] A. A. Abalkhail and S. M. Al Amri, "Saudi Arabia's Management of the Hajj Season through Artificial Intelligence and Sustainability," *Sustainability*, vol. 14, no. 21. 2022. doi: 10.3390/su142114142.

[16] A. J. Showail, "Solving Hajj and Umrah Challenges Using Information and Communication Technology: A Survey," *IEEE Access*, vol. 10, pp. 75404–75427, 2022, doi: 10.1109/ACCESS.2022.3190853.

[17] W. Van Der Aalst et al., "Process mining manifesto," in *Business Process Management Workshops: BPM 2011 International Workshops, Clermont-Ferrand, France, August 29, 2011, Revised Selected Papers, Part I 9*, Springer, 2012, pp. 169–194, https://doi.org/10.1007/978-3-642-28108-2_19

[18] H. M. W. Verbeek, J. Buijs, B. F. Van Dongen, and W. M. P. van der Aalst, "Prom 6: The process mining toolkit," *Proc. of BPM Demonstration Track*, vol. 615, pp. 34–39, 2010.

[19] C. W. Günther and A. Rozinat, "Disco: Discover Your Processes.," *BPM (Demos)*, vol. 940, no. 1, pp. 40–44, 2012, doi:https://api.semanticscholar.org/CorpusID:2907725

[20] "Celonis," 2015. https://www.celonis.com/ (accessed Jul. 06, 2023).

[21] A. J. M. M. Weijters and W. Van Der Aalst, "Process Mining with the Heuristics Miner-algorithm Process Mining over SAP Data View project Process Mining in Smart Homes View project," 2014. [Online]. Available: https://www.researchgate.net/publication/229124308

[22] Y. A. Effendi, R. Sarno, and D. V. Marsha, "Improved fuzzy miner algorithm for business process discovery," *Telkomnika (Telecommunication Computing Electronics and Control)*, vol. 19, no. 6, pp. 1830–1839, Dec. 2021, doi: 10.12928/TELKOMNIKA.v19i6.19015.

[23] A. Bogarín, R. Cerezo, and C. Romero, "Discovering learning processes using inductive miner: A case study with learning management systems (LMSs)," *Psicothema*, vol. 30, no. 3, pp. 322–329, 2018, doi: 10.7334/psicothema2018.116.

[24] A. Wang, A. Biswas, H. Admoni, and A. Steinfeld, "Towards Rich, Portable, and Large-Scale Pedestrian Data Collection," *arXiv preprint arXiv:2203.01974*, 2022.

[25] Z. Sun, J. Chen, L. Chao, W. Ruan, and M. Mukherjee, "A Survey of Multiple Pedestrian Tracking Based on Tracking-by-Detection Framework," *IEEE Transactions on Circuits and Systems for Video Technology*, vol. 31, no. 5. Institute of Electrical and Electronics Engineers Inc., pp. 1819–1833, May 01, 2021. doi: 10.1109/TCSVT.2020.3009717.

[26] J. Seidenschwarz, G. Brasó, V. C. Serrano, I. Elezi, and L. Leal-Taixé, "Simple Cues Lead to a Strong Multi-Object Tracker," Jun. 2022, [Online]. Available: http://arxiv.org/abs/2206.04656

[27] A. Alharbi, "Face Recognition for Multiple Visits Trajectory Detection," *submitted to Applied Sciences Journal*, 2023.

[28] I. Shugurov and A. A. Mitsyuk, "Generation of a set of event logs with noise," in *Proceedings of the Spring/Summer Young Researchers' Colloquium on Software Engineering* 2014,doi: 10.15514/SYRCOSE-2014-8-13

Computer Systems and Communication Technology
W. Zheng (Ed.)
© 2024 The Authors.
doi:10.3233/ATDE240004

Simulation Model for Economic Analysis of Shore Power Technique

Rong Fu[a,b], Jialing Li[a], Jia Zhu[b], Jie Yu[b], Jin Han[b], Yifan Tang[a,1]
[a] *School of Computer and Information, Three Gorges University*
[b] *State Grid Yichang Electric Power Supply Company*
ORCiD ID: Jialing Li https://orcid.org/0009-0001-0118-5970

Abstract. Maritime vessels utilizing shore power while docked offer significant potential for substantial reduction of exhaust emissions, consequently mitigating atmospheric pollution within port environs. However, the substantial initial investment costs associated with constructing shore power infrastructure and retrofitting vessels with shore power access equipment pose a substantial challenge, as the short-term economic returns are not readily apparent. This unfavorable aspect significantly impedes the widespread adoption of shore power technology. Furthermore, dynamic factors such as government subsidy policies, environmental mandates for maritime vessels, electricity pricing, fuel costs, and port queuing strategies exert direct influence over the economic returns of shore power systems, thereby introducing significant complexities into the comprehensive evaluation of their economic viability. In response to these challenges, this paper presents a simulation model designed to replicate the behaviors of vessels, shore power facilities, and dynamic factors. This model offers a detailed estimation of the economic benefits of shore power systems throughout their entire lifecycle under various operational strategies. The simulation model is implemented using the Anylogic tool. The results indicate that the simulation outcomes over the past three years closely align with actual data, thus affirming the reliability of the model. The simulation model serves as a valuable decision-making tool for vessel operators, shore power stakeholders, and governmental authorities. It is conducive to the promotion of shore power adoption and enables the projection of the economic benefits of shore power systems over a defined time horizon.

Keywords. Shore power system, anyLogic simulation, economic benefits, maritime vessels, port

1. Introduction

Presently, China's port infrastructure for shore power systems is well-established, with various ports having the capability to provide shore power to different types of vessels. However, the utilization rate of shore power facilities in Chinese ports remains exceedingly low. In 2019, 29 coastal and 19 inland ports reported shore power usage [1] data to the Ministry of Transport's Maritime Bureau. Throughout the year, approximately 1,088 berths utilized shore power for around 60,000 occurrences, totaling approximately 740,000 hours of power supply and 45 million kilowatt-hours of electricity. For instance, a major coastal port invested ¥63.54 million over 2015-2018

---

[1] Corresponding Author: Yifan Tang, 1921038166@qq.com.

in constructing six high-capacity shore power supply systems. However, by the end of 2018, only eight vessels berthing at the port had utilized shore power[5]. Low adoption rates can be attributed to the high economic costs associated with shore power. For instance, the annual cost of a ferry using shore power at the Gothenburg port was 26.7% higher than generating power with auxiliary engines[3]. Similarly, for ocean-going vessels berthing in Chinese coastal ports, shore power was 62.5% to 150% more expensive than auxiliary engine power generation[4]. Such cost disparities significantly affect the willingness of vessels to adopt shore power. To address this, both central and local governments have implemented various subsidy policies, such as reducing electricity prices for shore power, reducing port shore power service fees, partially subsidizing shore power system retrofits, and levying environmental protection taxes. Shore power systems encompass port electrical supply facilities, which generate revenue through shore power service fees, and vessel electrical receiving facilities, which use shore power instead of auxiliary engines to save costs and protect the environment.

Given the aforementioned context, the analysis of the economic benefits of ships adopting shore power systems is of paramount importance, particularly in light of relevant policies. Current methods of assessing the economic benefits of shore power primarily fall into two categories: those emphasizing energy savings and those focusing on emission reduction. The former assess the cost savings in energy consumption when vessels use shore power instead of auxiliary generators, while the latter examine the emission reduction benefits of shore power compared to auxiliary generator operation[6-8].

Existing research methods tend to lack systematic and comprehensive analyses. Although single-factor and scenario analyses reveal the impact of subsidies, environmental protection tax levies, and changes in individual factors, they often overlook that factors such as electricity prices, fuel costs, fuel quality, shore power maintenance costs, and environmental protection taxes are subject to dynamic variations. These dynamic factors can lead to inaccurate analysis results. Additionally, most existing methods do not consider the variations in shore power facilities and power supply services in different ports, which could yield different results if these variations were taken into account.

To address these limitations, this paper introduces a simulation model for the economic analysis of shore power systems. This model incorporates the evolving factors, such as electricity prices and fuel costs, and offers a more comprehensive economic benefits assessment. Furthermore, it considers the entire cost and revenue lifecycle of shore power systems, from retrofitting to usage, using the Anylogic simulation software to construct the shore power system and related port facilities. It visualizes different operating states of shore power systems, explores the impact of changing factors on the economic benefits of shore power under different scenarios, and promotes the adoption of shore power technology.

2. Related Work

Traditional methods of economic benefit analysis for shore power systems have predominantly employed cost analysis, comparative analysis, and factor analysis. Several scholars have conducted related studies, such as Tao Xuezong et al.[13], who considered policies like subsidies for shore power system retrofitting and usage, as well as environmental protection tax measures. They improved the cost comparison method using a cash flow analysis and developed an economic analysis model for vessels adopting shore power. Using a typical container ship berthed at the Shanghai Yangshan Third Phase Terminal as a case study, they empirically analyzed auxiliary engine power generation costs, shore power usage costs, and benefits under various scenarios. They also investigated the impact of a ship's remaining lifespan on shore power economic indicators and the latest retrofit year through annual comparisons. Additionally, factor analysis revealed the effects of various policy and non-policy factors on shore power economic indicators. Lai Danhong et al.[14] considered the economic aspects of shore power technology at ports and for vessels. They comprehensively assessed port investment costs, port cost recovery periods, vessel investment costs, vessel cost recovery periods, and national subsidies. Through an analysis of the interplay and impact of these factors, they substantiated the economic feasibility of shore power technology.Feng Hua et al.[15] used a coastal port's shore power operational system as an example. They considered port economic factors, a model comparing costs before and after shore power retrofit, as well as the impact of shore power service fees and berth utilization rates influenced by internet technology. They assessed factors affecting the post-retrofit fuel efficiency payback period and port cost recovery period. Their study confirmed the feasibility of shore power operation, showing that selecting appropriate shore power service fees and achieving optimal berth utilization rates could lead to noticeable economic benefits for ports and vessel operators over a certain timeframe.Nevertheless, without the follow-up of national policies and subsidies, it is insufficient to promote shore power systems rapidly solely through the efforts of ports and vessel operators. The lack of adequate subsidies presents a significant barrier to the widespread adoption of shore power technology.Di Zhongjie[17] and others focused on studying the interactive mechanisms among government entities, port enterprises, and shipping companies regarding shore power system strategy choices. They discussed the impact of shore power implementation on the evolutionary stable strategies of multiple stakeholders using an evolutionary game theory model.Zhao Jingxian et al.[16] proposed a two-stage game model between ports and vessels, simulating the dynamic game process between both parties, aiming to assist ports in determining the optimal number of shore power retrofitted berths and the corresponding shore power service fees while safeguarding vessel interests and autonomy.

The aforementioned studies comprehensively consider various factors influencing the adoption of shore power systems from both the vessel and port perspectives. They incorporate the effects of relevant policies and establish economic benefit calculation models, thoroughly demonstrating the economic viability of vessels adopting shore power systems. However, these studies do not account for the dynamic nature of multiple factors affecting shore power economic benefits, such as electricity prices, fuel costs, and maintenance expenses. This paper's economic benefit assessment model offers a more comprehensive approach, basing its calculations on historical shore power system operation data, utilizing AnyLogic as a development tool to construct a shore power simulation system, and validating the economic benefit model.

3. Assessment Model

3.1. Comprehensive Model

To facilitate the research, taking into account the status of the construction and usage of shore power facilities in Chinese ports and the rules governing shore power usage, the following assumptions are presented: ports are equipped with shore power facilities, and their electrical supply capacity is abundant, sufficient to meet the electricity demand of vessels upon docking.The vessels have a lifespan of N years.The retrofitting of the shore power system does not affect the vessels' lifespan, cargo capacity, fuel consumption rate, or other parameters.During a vessel's port stay, the use of shore power is not mandated and can be chosen based on practical considerations.The economic benefits of using shore power by vessels take into account policy subsidies and the collection of environmental protection taxes.

Typically, when vessels use shore power during port stays, a service fee is levied. Ports aim to collect relatively high shore power service fees while incurring minimal costs for berth retrofitting, in order to maximize their own revenue. However, in many cases, vessels opt to use their own auxiliary generators for power due to the higher costs associated with shore power. The entire process can be described in two stages. In the first stage, the port decides which berths to retrofit with shore power and establishes the shore power service fee based on the vessels' port call circumstances, with the aim of maximizing revenue. In the second stage, vessel companies determine whether to use shore power based on their individual considerations, which include power requirements, the efficiency of their auxiliary generators in converting fuel to electricity, the duration of their stay in the port, as well as the prevailing fuel prices and shore power service fees at that time. The overall model is depicted in Figure 1, where 'n' represents the total number of vessels in the port.

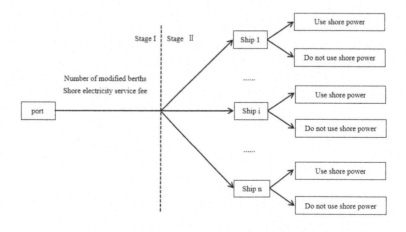

Figure 1. Two-Stage Model Structure Diagram

3.2. The cost of shore power utilization by vessels

Upon choosing to utilize shore power, vessels require a period to connect to the land-based power source. During this connection process, vessels continue to use auxiliary generators for power supply. Consequently, the vessel's electricity cost encompasses the paid shore power service fee, the fuel cost during land-based power connection, waiting time expenses, and any levied environmental protection taxes. Assuming the vessel has a remaining service life of N years, and the shore power system retrofit begins at the start of the year and is completed within a year.The overall cost calculation formula is expressed as follows[2].

$$Q^i_{ele} = \sum_{n=1}^{N} [\pi_{ser} P_i(t_i - t_f) + \pi_{oil} P t_f \omega_i + \phi_i T^i_{ele} + P_i t_f \sum_{j=1}^{s} (\beta_j r_j)] \tag{1}$$

In the equation provided:
n represents the annual time index within the remaining lifespan of the vessel.
n represents the annual time index within the remaining lifespan of the vessel.
N is the remaining lifespan of the vessel (in years).

π_{ser} is the service fee for shore power.

P_i is the charging power for vessel i.

t_i is the total time the ship is berthed.

t_f is the time required to connect the ship to shore power.

π_{oil} is the price of fuel.

φ_i is the cost coefficient for waiting time of the ship.

T^i_{ele} is the waiting time in the queue for ship i to use shore power.

j represents different types of pollutants, includes the main pollutants, such as SO_x (sulfur oxides) and NO_x (nitrogen oxides).

s is the total amount of pollutants intended to be emitted.

β_j is the emission factor for compliant fuel (g/(kW h)).

r_j is the environmental pollution tax rate for pollutant j (rmb/kg).

ω_i represents the conversion efficiency of the ship's auxiliary generator from fuel to electricity.

3.3. Cost of Ship Auxiliary Generator Utilization

If a ship opts to employ an auxiliary generator to provide power to the ship's electrical system during its berthing period, the resultant costs encompass waiting time costs, fuel expenditures, environmental protection taxes, and maintenance costs for the auxiliary generator. Q_{oil}^i represents the total cost of using auxiliary generators for the entire remaining lifespan of the ship during its berthing periods[2]:

$$Q_{oil}^i = \sum_{n=1}^{N} [\phi_i T_{oil}^i + \pi_{oil} P t_i \omega_i + P t_i \sum_{j=1}^{s} (\beta_j r_j) + M_n]$$

(2)

In the equation, φ_i is the waiting time cost coefficient for the ship, T_{oil}^i is the total queue time for fueling the ship, π_{oil} is the fuel price, β_j is the emission factor for compliant fuel (g/(kW h)), and r_j is the environmental pollution tax rate for the j-th emission category (RMB/kg). Lastly, M_n represents the maintenance cost of the auxiliary generator during the berthing period in the n-th year.

By computing the difference between the total cost of using shore power and the total cost of using auxiliary generators, one can determine the economic feasibility of ships when retrofitting shore power systems and using them to a certain extent[1].

$$\Delta Q = Q_{ele}^i - Q_{oil}^i$$

(3)

In the equation: ΔQ represents the economic indicator of using shore power for ships, referred to as the shore power economic indicator. A positive value indicates better economic viability, while a negative value suggests that it lacks economic viability.

3.4. The costs generated by the port

The costs incurred by the port primarily include the renovation expenses of the shore power system, electricity charges paid, and the maintenance costs of the shore power system. The calculation formula is as follows[2]:

$$Q_g = kC(1-\theta) + \pi_e \sum_{i=1}^{m} P_i(t_i - t_f) Y_i + W_n$$

(4)

In the formula: k represents the number of shore power berths the port invests in renovation. C signifies the cost invested in renovating a single shore power berth. θ stands for the government's subsidy rate for renovating shore power. π_e denotes the electricity price from shore power. m represents the total number of ships. W_n is the annual maintenance cost of the shore power system for year 'n' (in thousands of RMB).Yi=1 indicates a ship using shore power.Yi=0 signifies a ship not using shore power.

3.5. The revenue generated by the port

The port's revenue includes the service fees paid by ships for using shore power, which is related to the quantity of shore power used and the port's pricing. The calculation formula is as follows[2]:

$$R_g = \pi_{ser} \sum_{i=1}^{m} P_i(t_i - t_f)Y_i \tag{5}$$

In conclusion, for the port to achieve maximum revenue, the variables are the number of shore power berth conversions and the shore power service fees. The maximum benefit for the port can be expressed as follows[2]:

$$\max(R_g - Q_g) \tag{6}$$

3.6. The simulation methods

In this article, the simulation and modeling were conducted using the simulation software, AnyLogic. The modeling process primarily comprises two distinct phases: the construction of agent-based models and the setup of the simulation environment.Construction of Agent-Based Models: Agent attributes were primarily defined by leveraging parameters and variables from the agent library.Agent states were established using statecharts and functions.Setup of the Simulation Environment:Importation of a simulation map.Path definition within the simulation scenario was carried out using spatial mark-up components from the modeling library. Parameters within the simulation environment were set using variables.The connection between intelligent agents and the simulation environment was established to enable simulation visualization on the main interface. This facilitated subsequent processes of simulation validation and experimentation. The model construction process is illustrated in Figure 2.

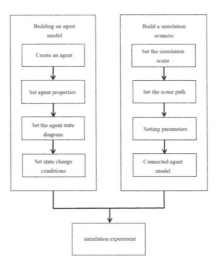

Figure 2. Simulation Model Development Process

4. Simulation Experimentation Process and Conclusions

4.1. Maritime Vessel Berthing Process

Upon the arrival of vessels at the port, they proceed to enter the harbor and berth at the dock, selecting an appropriate power supply method based on the actual circumstances. Taking into consideration the vessel's entry and exit processes at the port and the requirements of simulation experiments, the process of vessel entry into the port is constructed as depicted in Figure 3.

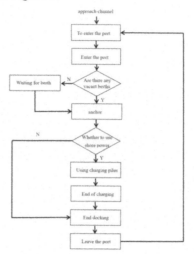

Figure 3. Ship Arrival Flowchart

In accordance with the vessel berthing process, upon a vessel's arrival at the port, it follows a prescribed navigational route to enter the harbor. If no berths are available, the vessel must wait until one becomes vacant. Upon securing a berth, the vessel selects its power supply mode. In the event of choosing shore-based electrical power supply, it connects to charging stations for recharging. After the berthing period concludes, the vessel departs the port and navigates back out through the designated channel.

The process diagram for vessel charging at the charging stations is illustrated in Figure 4. When the ship needs to use the charging pile to charge, it is necessary to stop the ship at the designated position. The staff starts to connect the charging pile with the ship, start the charging procedure, and start charging. When the charging is finished, the connection between the charging pile and the ship will be disconnected, and the ship can leave the charging pile and continue other operations or navigation plans.

Figure 4. Flow Chart of Ship Charging Process

Figure. 4 depicts the complete process of the ship from the start of charging to the end of charging, including the steps of ensuring the ship to berth, connecting the charging pile, starting charging, disconnecting the charging pile after charging, etc.

4.2. Parameter Selection

Under typical circumstances, the average duration for vessels to connect to shore-based electrical power is 60 minutes (tf=1h), and the expected lifespan of shore-based electrical charging stations is approximately 30 years. In terms of auxiliary generators, the cost per kilowatt-hour ranges from 0.98 to 1.14 rmb. Conversely, when employing a shore-based electrical power system, the cost per kilowatt-hour falls between 0.52 and 1.12 rmb. According to the regulations set forth by the Maritime Administration of the Ministry of Transport, vessels entering China's inland emission control areas are prohibited from utilizing fuel with a sulfur content exceeding 0.1%. Hence, this study adopts a low-sulfur oil price of 3100 rmb per ton. The primary emissions and their respective pollution equivalence values for the use of low-sulfur oil are detailed in Table 1, with a gas pollutant fee rate of 7 rmb per pollution equivalent[15].

Table 1. Emission Factors for Pollutants and Their Equivalents

Pollutant Names	Emission Factor (g.kWh-1)	Equivalent Emissions (kg)
SO2	0.492	0.95
CO	1.100	16.70
CO2	683.000	5000.00
NOX	12.220	0.95
PM10	0.300	4.00

4.3. Simulation Process

The simulation model employs the behavioral simulation of vessel agents to depict the vessel berthing process. Within the AnyLogic simulation software, the behavior of these agents is defined through statecharts in the agent library. By associating distinct vessel actions with various states of the vessel agent, specific agent rules and transition conditions are established based on the vessel's port entry process. This facilitates the construction of logical models for vessel berthing and for the use of shore-based electrical charging stations, as illustrated in Figures 5 and 6. These figures represent the statecharts of vessel agents and charging station usage, respectively, designed within the AnyLogic software for this study.

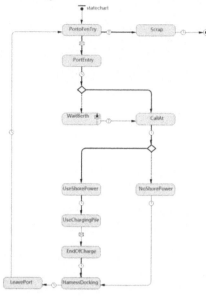

Figure 5. The state chart for the AnyLogic vessel agent

Explanatory Notes on Statechart Transition Logic:

The transition from "Awaiting Entry to Port" state to "Entering Port" state. When the port accepts a vessel's entry, it transmits an "arrive" message to the vessel. Upon receiving the message, the vessel transitions from the "Awaiting Entry into Harbor" state to the "Entering Harbor" state and guides the vessel to an awaiting anchorage point.

The transition from "Entering Harbor" state to "Waiting for berth or Berthed" state. Upon entering the harbor, an assessment is made regarding berth availability. If vacant berths are present, the vessel proceeds to the berthing point; otherwise, it continues to remain at the anchorage point, awaiting a berth.

The transition from "Waiting for berth" state to "Berthed" state. Vessels in the 'Awaiting Berth' state monitor messages, and upon receiving a 'Departure' message from vessels leaving the port, they verify the availability of vacant berths. If vacant berths are found, they transition to the 'Berthed' state.

The transition from "Berthed" state to "Using Shore-Based Electrical Power" state. berthing phase, if a vessel is identified as electrically retrofitted, the port automatically locates a vacant berth equipped with available charging stations, proceeds to connect to shore-based electrical power, and transitions into the ' Using Shore-Based Electrical Power ' state."

The transition from "Using Shore-Based Electrical Power" state to "Utilizing Charging Stations" state. When a vessel is connected to the charging station, it enters the "Using Charging Station" state. It then sends a usage message to the corresponding charging station, causing the charging station to transition from an idle state to a usage state.

The transition from "Utilizing Charging Stations" state to "Charging Completion" state. When the vessel completes berthing, the charging state ends. After disconnecting from the charging station, the charging station will send instructions to the vessel, and the vessel's state changes to "Charging Completion."

The transition from "Charging Completion" state to "Berth stop with a cable harness" state. When the vessel disconnects from the charging station, the vessel enters the cable harness stop state.

The transition from "Berth stop with a cable harness" state to "Leaving the port" state. When the vessel's stop is complete, it automatically transitions to the "Leaving the port" state.

The transition from "Leaving the port" state to "Awaiting entry to the port" state. After the vessel departs from the port, after some time, it will return to the port and transition to the "Awaiting entry to the port" state.

The transition from "Berthed" state to "Not using shore power" state. When a vessel is in the berthed state, the port will check if the vessel has been retrofitted for electrical power use. If not, the port will automatically find an available berth. After that, the vessel transitions to the "Not using shore power" state.

The transition from "Not using shore power" state to " Line handling" state. Once the vessel arrives at the berth, it will transition to the "Line handling" state.

The transition from " Awaiting entry to the port" state to "Scrapped" state. Before a vessel enters the port, its status is checked to determine if it has been scrapped. If it is in a scrapped state, it transitions to a termination state.

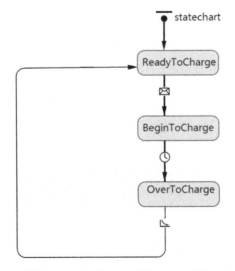

Figure 6. The state chart for vessel charging within AnyLogic

Description of transition logic of state diagram:

When the ship needs to use the charging pile to charge, the ship should be parked at the designated position, and the staff began to connect the charging pile with the ship and start the charging procedure. Start charging. When the charging is finished, the connection between the charging pile and the ship will be disconnected, and the ship can leave the charging pile and continue other operations or navigation plans.

The simulation model utilizes the waterways along the main channel of Yichang Port in Yichang City, Hubei Province, as well as anchorages and berths within the port area as the non-agent-based simulation environment. The main display interface (main) imports the bottom map of Yichang Port with a set scale of 1:10 (meters: pixels), and the construction of the waterway network is completed. The simulated scene of Yichang Port is shown in Figures 7, 8, and 9. Upon running the model and entering the main view, it displays harbor points and vessels generated based on externally provided port information and vessel information files. Vessels move according to their trajectory information. When a vessel arrives at the port, clicking on the port allows entry into the port view, where information about the port and charging stations is available. Upon entering the port, the system checks berth availability. If a berth is available, the vessel enters the berthing state. If the vessel is electric and there are charging stations available, it will connect to the charging station. If all berths are occupied, the vessel will remain in the waiting state until a berth becomes vacant. Once cargo unloading is completed, vessels depart from the port automatically. After a certain period, they will re-enter the port.

Figure 7. Simulated scenario of the Yichang area

Figure 7 shows the geographical scope of the simulation experiment scene, including the main landmarks and navigation channels in Yichang City, Hubei Province. The red dot in the figure 1. Identifies the specific scope of the simulation scene, and 2. Identifies the location of Yichang Port.

Figure 8. Simulated scenario of Yichang Port

Figure 8 shows the specific situation of Yichang port area in the simulation experiment of this paper, including key information such as entry channel, berth distribution, shore wall and so on. In the figure, 1 identifies the approach channel and 2 identifies the specific berth.

calcLightPrice	SO1	allPriceCost
calcOilPrice	SO2	waitconnectTime
yearOilCollection	CO1	oilPrice
yearPowerCollection	CO2	lightPrice
oilPowerPriceFile	NO1	chargingPileConnectionTime
calcMax	NO2	beginChargingPileTime
getNowPrice	PM1	endChargingPileTime
getNowYear	PM2	modelBeginTime
	CO21	sewageCosts
	CO22	timeCostRate
	name	waitTimeAllCost
	isOild	chargingPileOne
	type	shipTime
		allTime
		beginTime
		endTime
		chargingTime
		intoWaitTime
		stopWaitTime
		msg
		isOk

harbor   main

connections

Figure 9. Simulation experiment parameters

Figure 9 lists the main parameters and values used in the simulation experiment, including ship parameters and policy scenario parameters.

In order to reveal the impact patterns of changing factors such as electricity prices, fuel prices, and environmental protection taxes on the economic benefits of ship usage of shore power systems, the economic benefits throughout the lifecycle of ships are calculated based on fluctuating fuel prices and shore power prices during different time periods.

A single ship's economic benefits are simulated for a single port call, and the economic benefits of a single ship using shore power and fuel are calculated separately. The parameter values are as follows:

Table 2. Vessel parameters

Parameters	Values	Equivalent Emissions (kg)
Vessel charging power	65	kW.h
Fuel price	10	RMB/L
Queue time to enter the port	80	Minutes
Fuel-to-electricity conversion ratio.	50%	—
Vessel berthing time	603	Minutes

Table 3. Economic benefits of a single vessel

Power supply mode	Economic benefit (/rmb).
Auxiliary generator power supply	2049
Shore power supply	2449.15

The economic benefits for ships during a single port call were calculated, and it is evident that the economic viability of using shore power after a ship docks is better than using auxiliary generators. However, this calculation does not consider the continuous fluctuations in fuel and electricity prices over the entire lifecycle of a ship. The factors influencing economic benefits are interrelated, and the retrofitting of shore power systems on ships requires an initial investment. Therefore, the simulation was conducted to assess the economic benefits of different types of ships over their entire lifecycle. Due to the relatively high initial cost of retrofitting shore power systems on ships, government subsidies are required to balance economic benefits and encourage ship usage of shore power.

Table 4. Economic benefits across the entire lifecycle for different types of vessels

Ship Types	Remaining Lifespan After Shore Power Retrofit (years)	Economic Benefit of Using Shore Power After Retrofit (in 10,000 RMB)	Economic Benefit of Using Auxiliary Generators Without Retrofit (in 10,000 RMB)	Government Subsidy Required (in 10,000 RMB)
Cargo Ship	20	349.3	245.8	103.5
Fishing Boat	15	215.7	114.9	100.8
Cruise Ship	19	578.1	376.6	201.5

Using AnyLogic simulation software, 100 ships of the same type were simulated for shore power retrofitting at the same time. These ships had remaining lifetimes ranging from 1 to 20 years. To maintain the total number of ships, the retiring ships were replaced with new ones. The simulation allowed for tracking the economic benefits of ships with different remaining lifetimes. Fluctuations in electricity and fuel prices during different time periods were considered, and different numbers of ships were simulated for shore power retrofitting based on specific ratios to determine the overall economic benefits for the 100 ships. This analysis was used to identify the most appropriate number of charging stations for port-side retrofitting.

Table 5. Overall Economic Benefits for 100 Ships

Number of Ships Using Auxiliary Generators (/vessel)	Number of Ships Using Shore Power (/vessel)	Economic Benefits (in 10,000 CNY)	Number of Charging Stations
0	100	9695.4	23
10	90	9051.7	23
20	80	8425.9	22
30	70	7786.2	20
40	60	7150.9	18
50	50	6538.3	15
60	40	5907.7	13
70	30	5276.1	10
80	20	4664.7	6
90	10	4022.8	4
100	0	3392.1	0

To reveal the impact patterns of subsidies and environmental taxes on the economic indicators of shore power, a baseline scenario (Scenario 0) was set as not imposing environmental taxes and not providing subsidies for shore power system retrofitting and usage. Based on this baseline, seven policy scenarios were established by considering whether subsidies for shore power usage and shore power system retrofitting were provided and whether environmental taxes were imposed. The explanations for the baseline scenario and the seven policy scenarios are provided in Table 6. The simulation model proposed in this paper was utilized to calculate the economic benefits of shore power in different scenarios.

Table 6. Explanation of Scenario Settings

Scenario	Shore Power Usage Subsidy (CNY/kW.h)	Shore Power System Retrofit Subsidy	Number of Charging Stations
1	0.4	0	0
2	0	25%	0
3	0.4	25%	0
4	0	0	8
5	0.4	0	9
6	0	25%	0.55

Table 7. Electricity Costs for Ships During Port Stay in Different Scenarios

Power Supply Method	Scenario	Annual Total (in 10,000 CNY)	One-time Port Call (in 10,000 CNY)	Per Kilowatt-Hour (in CNY)
Auxiliary Generator	0、1、2、3	275	5.5	0.98
	4、5、6	360	6	1.14
Shore Power	0	284	5	1.02
	1	260	5	0.9
	2	297	5	1.01
	3	235	5	0.85
	4	357	6	1.18
	5	267	5	0.95
	6	352	6	1.16

5. Conclusion and Outlook

In this study, a simulation model of economic benefit analysis of shore power technology is proposed, which considers the influencing factors of dynamic change and can estimate the economic benefit of the whole life cycle of shore power system under different strategies. study found:

In the absence of government intervention, the cost of using shore power exceeds that of traditional auxiliary power generation after mobilizing environmental tax.

For the government, the non-compulsory shore power sovereignty is the key. The combination of shore power sovereignty and environmental tax is more conducive to the adoption of shore power by ships.

The simulation experiment predicts the economic balance point between ships and ports in the next 10 years.

Although the data limitation effect of the model includes all factors, its verification on a small data set is consistent with the reality. Future research will consider the difference between shore power facilities and power supply services, so as to improve the prediction accuracy of the model and explore the social benefits of ships using shore power, and may also be extended to other routes.

ACKNOWLEDGMENTS

This work is supported by State Grid Yichang Company Management Technology Project :B715H023XT08.

References

[1]   Hu JY, Gu Q, Liu Q. Application Practice of Shore Power Technology for Chongqing-Three Gorges Cruise [J]. Waterway Engineering, 2021 (09): 76-80+100.doi: 10.16233/J.CNKI.ISSN 1002-4972.10001.10001000016.

[2]   Peng CS. An empirical analysis of the application of shore power technology for ships at ports abroad [J]. Port Economy, 2012 (11): 11-14.doi:CNKI:SUN:GKJJ.0.2012-11-005.

[3]   He H, Xu ZH, Xie ZG. Research and application of ship shore power monitoring system [J]. China Waterway, 2022 (04): 84-87. doi:10.13646/J.CN.KI.42-1395/U.2022.04.028.

[4]   Liu C, Tang WW, Yao JX. A comprehensive review of the technical application and development of shore power systems at domestic and foreign ports [J]. Water Transportation Engineering, 2020, 0(5): 173-176234.doi:10.16233/j.cnki.issn1002-4972.20200509.044.

[5]   Liu D, Sun JX, Qiao KH, et al. Overview of research on shore power supply system of port ships [J]. Ship Power Technology, 2021,41 (06): 29-34.doi:10.13632/j.meee.2021.06.010.

[6]   Huo WQ, Fu W, Xu GL, et al. Analysis of port shore power technology and its promotion [J]. Energy and Energy Conservation, 2017 (2): 2-5.doi:10.16643/j.cnki.14-1360/td.2017.02.001.

[7]   Lai DH, Chen WW, Huang WT, et al. Economic analysis of shore power technology [J]. Port Technology, 2016, 53 (3): 57-62.doi:10.16403/j.cnki.ggjs20160315.

[8]   Tseng PH, Pilcher N. A study of the potential of shore power for the port of Kaohsiung, Taiwan: to introduce or not to introduce? [J]. Research in Transportation Business & Management, 2015, 17: 83-91.doi:10.1016/j.rtbm.2015.09.001.

[9]   Ballini F, Bozzo R. Air pollution from ships in ports: the socioeconomic benefit of cold-ironing technology [J]. Research in Transportation Business & Management, 2015, 17: 92-98.doi:10.1016/j.rtbm.2015.10.007.

[10] Innes A, Monios J. Identifying the unique challenges of installing cold ironing at small and medium ports: the case of Aberdeen [J]. Transportation Research Part D: Transport and Environment, 2018, 62: 298-313.doi:10.1016/j.trd.2018.02.004.

[11] Yu J, Voss S, Tang G. Strategy development for retrofitting ships for implementing shore side electricity [J]. Transportation Research Part D: Transport and Environment, 2019, 74: 201-213.doi:10.1016/j.trd.2019.08.004.

[12] Lai DH, Chen WW, Huang WT, et al. Economic analysis of shore power technology [J]. Port Technology, 2016, 53(03): 57-62. doi:10.16403/j.cnki.ggjs20160315.

[13] Zhou T. Application and development of wharf shore power system technology at home and abroad [J]. Port Engineering Technology, 2023,60 (03): 41-44.doi:10.16403/j.cnki.ggjs 20230310.

[14] Lang X, Zhongjie D, Jihong C, et al. Evolutionary game analysis on behavior strategies of multiple stakeholders in maritime shore power system [J]. Ocean and Coastal Management, 2021, 202.doi:10.1016/J.OCECOAMAN.2020.105508.

[15] Tan XL. Research on emergency evacuation of ships based on Anylogic [D]. Jimei University, 2023. doi:10.27720/d.cnki.gjmdx.2022.000168.

Computer Systems and Communication Technology
W. Zheng (Ed.)
© 2024 The Authors.
This article is published online with Open Access by IOS Press and distributed under the terms
of the Creative Commons Attribution Non-Commercial License 4.0 (CC BY-NC 4.0).
doi:10.3233/ATDE240005

Research on Monocular Vision Target Detection and Localization Under Non-Orthographic Conditions

Yahua Wu [a], Yuqing Chen [a,1] and Wei Yu [a]

[a] *College of Marine Electrical Engineering, Dalian Maritime University, Dalian 116026*

ORCiD ID: Wei Yu   https://orcid.org/0009-0002-1086-8439

Abstract. Aiming at the target localization problem in monocular vision, this paper proposes a nonlinear target localization method under non-orthoptic conditions. First, an image is captured using a monocular camera and a network framework based on YOLOv7 is constructed to detect the target in the image. Then, based on the principle of aperture imaging, the imaging models of orthophoto and non-orthophoto are established, and the nonlinear relationship between pixel coordinates and world coordinates in the image is deduced, so as to calculate the relative position coordinates of the target. In order to verify the validity of this nonlinear imaging model, we choose different shapes and numbers of ship targets for verification. The experimental results show that the target localization accuracy of monocular vision can reach more than 90% under non-orthoptic conditions.

Keywords. YOLOv7, non-orthophoto, target detection, monocular vision, target location

1. Introduction

With the rapid development of computers, communications, sensing and other technologies, the level of various computer vision technologies and applications is also increasing. After years of development, computer vision has developed different fields according to practical needs, such as image classification [1], target detection [2], instance segmentation [3], image semantic understanding [4], stereoscopic vision and 3D reconstruction [5].

Most existing monocular visual positioning methods assume that the target object and monocular camera are orthogonal. In this case, the pixel coordinates of the target object are linearly related to the world coordinates. However, in most application scenarios, when the pixel coordinates and world coordinates of the target object are no longer in a simple linear relationship, the observation angles of the camera and target object will appear non orthogonal. Based on this issue, this article proposes to establish a monocular camera imaging model under non orthogonal conditions, and introduces the concept of angle increment to complete the positioning of the target object.

---

[1] Corresponding Author: Yuqing Chen, chen@dlmu.edu.cn.

Target detection is the basis of target localization, and the detection accuracy directly affects the final localization results. In this paper, YOLOv7 [6] network will be used for pre-acquisition target detection.

2. Target localization model construction

2.1 Orthographic localization model

Considering the imaging model with the camera angle and the target satisfying the orthographic, shown in Figure 1. d_n denotes the distance between the object and the camera, and S_n denotes half of the maximum distance that can be captured in the horizontal direction of the camera when the distance is in a distance of d_n from the camera.

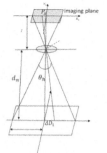

Figure 1. Orthorectified imaging model

Based on the similarity-similarity triangle principle, the following relationship can be introduced:

$$\frac{S_n}{d_n} = \frac{\frac{1}{2} \cdot N_D \cdot P_x}{f} = \tan\frac{\theta_h}{2} \tag{1}$$

where P_x is the physical width of each pixel on the sensor, N_D is the maximum number of pixels on the horizontal axis of the sensor. f is the focal length of the camera, and θ_h is the horizontal field-of-view angle of the camera. The actual physical width corresponding to a single pixel block when the target is at a distance d_n from the camera can also be derived from the similar triangle as:

$$\Delta D_n = \frac{2 \times \tan\frac{\theta_h}{2} \times d_n}{N_D} \tag{2}$$

The computation of vertical target localization is similar to that of the horizontal direction, i.e:

$$\Delta H_n = \frac{2 \times \tan\frac{\theta_v}{2} \times d_n}{N_H} \tag{3}$$

N_H is the maximum number of pixels of the sensor on the vertical axis, and θ_v is the vertical field of view of the camera. In this way, the actual physical length of a single pixel at a distance of d_1 from the camera corresponds to ΔH_n.

2.2 Non-orthographic localization model

The actual physical width corresponding to each pixel in the horizontal and vertical directions in the image is different from that in the orthorectified case under the camera shooting angle and the target in the non-orthorectified condition. A schematic diagram of the relationship between the parameters of the non-orthorectified camera imaging model is established, as shown in Figure 2.

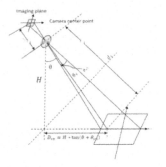

Figure 2. Non-orthorectified imaging model

where θ_v is the maximum vertical field of view of the camera, θ is the angle between the lower bound of the vertical field of view of the camera and the direction perpendicular to the ground, H is the height of the camera from the ground, and θ_{vn} ($n = 0,1,...N_H$) is the incremental angle due to the different pixel positions in the vertical direction. Therefore, the projection distance D_{vn} of different shooting distances d_n and camera height H can be further obtained by obtaining the incremental angles of different target positions, i.e.:

$$D_{vn} = H \times \tan\left(\theta + \theta_{vn}\right) \tag{4}$$

The target is diffused from the center of the optical axis to both sides, and the corresponding angular increment diffuses differently for each pixel frame, defining m as the pixel frame position. The corresponding angular distribution starts from the center of the sensor and defines this distribution as θ_m, as shown in Figure. 3.

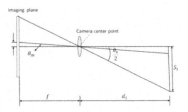

Figure 3. Schematic diagram of angle increment

According to the angular increment model parameter relationship in the figure, When $m= 1$, we can obtain:

$$\tan\theta_1 = \frac{P_x}{f} \tag{5}$$

When $m=N_H/2$, θ_m is 1/2 of the maximum vertical field of view, then we can obtain:

$$\frac{\theta_v}{2} = \tan^{-1}\left(\tan\theta_1 \times \frac{N_H}{2}\right) \tag{6}$$

Combining the above equations yields:

$$\theta_m = \tan^{-1}\left(m \times \frac{2 \times \tan\dfrac{\theta_v}{2}}{N_H}\right) \tag{7}$$

Considering the full view, the target spreads from the center of the optical axis to both sides, the incremental angle θ_{vn} is redefined as follows:

$$\theta_{vn} = \frac{\theta_v}{2} + \tan^{-1}\left(\left(n - \frac{N_H}{2}\right) \times \frac{2 \times \tan\dfrac{\theta_v}{2}}{N_H}\right) \tag{8}$$

Extending to the general case, the distance d_n satisfies:

$$d_n = \frac{H}{\cos\left(\theta + \theta_{vn}\right)} \tag{9}$$

Thus the coordinates in the horizontal direction are the product of the physical width ΔD_n of a single pixel and the number of pixels, which can be expressed as:

$$D_{hn} = p \times \frac{2 \times \tan\dfrac{\theta_d}{2} \times H}{N_D \times \cos\left(\theta + \theta_{vn}\right)}\left(-\frac{N_H}{2} \le p \le \frac{N_H}{2}\right) \tag{10}$$

By establishing the non-orthographic imaging model, the x,y-axis coordinates of the target relative to the camera sensor can be well described by Equation (4) and Equation (10) to complete the localization of the target.

3. Experimental results and analysis

3.1 Experimental results of monocular vision target localization

The experiment uses different numbers of ships on the sea surface as the target object for detection and localization, as shown in Figure 4.

(a)   (b)   (c)

Figure 4. Comparison of target detection results

The specific parameters and experimental results are shown in Table 1 for target localization according to the nonlinear localization model proposed in this paper under different heights and different tilt angles of the camera.

Table 1. Camera placement parameters and target localization results and system measurement errors before and after YOLOv7 improvement

Target number	1	2	3	4	5	6	7
Camera height (m)	2.7	4.5	4.5	3.6	3.6	3.6	3.6
Tilt angle Targeting	40	70	70	30	30	30	30
True Value (cm)	(-210,519)	(435,1189)	(-1277,3613)	(-166,209)	(139,323)	(-33,395)	(111,841)
Calculated values (cm)	(-199,511)	(424,1209)	(-1294,3605)	(-152,207)	(144,313)	(-35,381)	(102,855)
x-axis direction error	5.24%	2.53%	1.33%	8.43%	3.60%	7.14	8.11%
y-axis direction error	1.54%	1.68%	0.22%	0.96%	3.09%	3.54%	1.66%

According to the Table 1, the imaging model of monocular vision using Yolov7 and non-orthographic conditions can detect and localize different ships in different images, and the localization error is less than 8.43% in the x-axis direction and less than 3.54% in the y-axis direction overall. From this, it can be seen that the accuracy is above 90% in both the x-axis and y-axis directions

4. Conclusion

In this paper, a monocular visual target localization method under non-orthoptic conditions is proposed. First, target detection is performed based on Yolov7. Then, the nonlinear model of non-orthogonal monocular vision imaging is analyzed and established, and the relative position plane coordinates of the target under non-orthogonal conditions of monocular vision are inferred and calculated. In the experimental test, the accuracy of monocular vision localization under such non-orthogonal conditions can reach more than 90%.

References

[1] M. S. Patil and P. B. Mane, et al. Fused Image Classification using Pre-trained Deep Convolutional Neural Networks[C] Third International Conference on Artificial Intelligence and Smart Energy (ICAIS), Coimbatore, India, 2023: 1215-1221. doi: 10.1109/ICAIS56108.2023.10073743.

[2] W. Liu, M. Wang, S. Zhang and P. Zhou. Research on vehicle target detection technology based on UAV aerial images[C]//2022 IEEE International Conference on Mechatronics and Automation (ICMA), Guilin, Guangxi, China, 2022:412-416. doi: 10.1109/ICMA54519.2022.9856250.

[3] H. Dong and G. Wang, et al. DISF: Dynamic Instance Segmentation with Semantic Features[C]// 2022 26th International Conference on Pattern Recognition (ICPR), Montreal, QC, Canada, 2022: 3772-3778. doi: 10.1109/ICPR56361.2022.9956531.

[4] W. Zhou and L. Yu, et al. RFNet: Reverse Fusion Network with Attention Mechanism for RGB-D Indoor Scene Understanding[C]// IEEE Transactions on Emerging Topics in Computational Intelligence, 2023:598-603. doi: 10.1109/TETCI.2022.3160720.

[5] A. Islam, M. Asikuzzaman, M. O. Khyam, M. Noor-A-Rahim and M. R. Pickering. Stereo Vision-Based 3D Positioning and Tracking[J].2020: 138771-138787. doi: 10.1109/ACCESS.2020.3011360.

[6] Chien-Yao Wang and Alexey Bochkovskiy and H. Liao. YOLOv7: Trainable bag-of-freebies sets new state-of-the-art for real-time object detectors[J]. arXiv.org (2022):abs/2207.02696. doi: 10.48550/arXiv.2207.02696

Computer Systems and Communication Technology
W. Zheng (Ed.)
© 2024 The Authors.
This article is published online with Open Access by IOS Press and distributed under the terms
of the Creative Commons Attribution Non-Commercial License 4.0 (CC BY-NC 4.0).
doi:10.3233/ATDE240006

Heterogeneous Distributed Control Strategy for UAV-USV at Fixed-Time

XINMAN ZHANG [a], YUQING CHEN [a,1], WENLONG LU [a] and WEI YU [a]

[a] *College of Marine Electrical Engineering, Dalian Maritime University, Dalian 116026*

Abstract. Focusing on the collaborative control of quadrotor Unmanned Aerial Vehicles (UAVs) and underactuated Unmanned Surface Vessels (USVs), this article presents a cooperative control algorithm based on fixed-time theory. By constructing an adaptive neural network to approximate model uncertainty and unknown disturbances in the system, this algorithm satisfies the coordinated motion constraints between UAVs and USVs, while achieving group control objectives such as trajectory tracking. Additionally, this article employs the fixed-time method in the Lyapunov function to analyze system stability, ensuring that the cooperative control error converges within a fixed time, ultimately enabling fast and stable tracking of targets between UAVs and USVs. Finally, the effectiveness of the proposed algorithm is verified through numerical simulation experiments.

Keywords. Quadrotor; unmanned aerial vehicle; underactuated surface vessel; fixed-time theory; adaptive neural network.

1 Introduction

In recent years, the cooperative control technology between UAVs and USVs is a hot field of academic research and industrial application internationally [1]. A heterogeneous multi-intelligence body composed of UAVs and USVs with payload and mission configuration capabilities. UAVs can quickly reach the target area and provide real-time views, while USVs can perform precise maneuvering and acquisition tasks on the water surface. Through collaborative control, rapid response and efficient execution of the mis-sion can be realized. The UAV and USV are heterogeneous systems with different dy-namics models and state dimensions, so the first step is to solve the model heterogeneity problem. In this paper, the equivalent mapping technique is adopted to realize the coop-erative work. For UAV and USV systems, it is important to form the intended formation effect quickly, so the convergence speed is an important feature. In order to achieve faster convergence speed, fixed-time theory is used in this paper. A compensator-based com-mand filtering formation control algorithm based on fixed-time control theory and Lya-punov generalized function method are proposed in [2], so that the following submerged USV in any initial system state can track the leader in a given time. In the literature [3], a new non-singular fixed-time sliding-mode tracking controller is proposed to solve the fixed-time attitude tracking problem for the attitude coordinated control problem of a multi-spacecraft system with unknown external disturbances. For the problem of model uncertainty and external disturbance, in

---

[1] Corresponding Author: Yuqing Chen, e-mail: chen@dlmu.edu.cn

addition to designing observers and introducing fuzzy algorithms, the introduction of radial basis function neural networks is also and its common method [4]. Radial basis function neural networks are utilized to approximate the unknown dynamics of the UAV and USV and incorporated into the design of the controller [5]. In the literature [6], an improved adaptive control protocol for RBF neu-ral networks is designed by combining the advantages of adaptive techniques and radial basis function neural networks (RBF), which greatly reduces the number of unknown parameters that need to be updated. The main contributions of this paper include: (1) In addressing the heterogeneous system, we incorporate the equivalent mapping technique to transmit the planar position information from the UAV to the USV. (?) On the RBF-NN, we use the minimum parameter method. This inclusion serves to decrease the computational load associated with the system's network parameters. (3) In the stability proof, we introduce the fixed-time stability theory as an augmentation. This ensures the convergence of our heterogeneous multi-intelligence system within a fixed time frame.

2 Preparatory knowledge and problem description

2.1 Mathematical modeling of UAV and USV based on Eulerian- Lagrange forms

Based on the Euler-Lagrange model description method, the dynamics model of UAV [6]can be generally described as:

$$\begin{cases} \ddot{x}_a = (\cos\phi_a \sin\theta_a \cos\psi_a + \sin\phi_a \sin\psi_a)u_1 / m_a - k_x \dot{x}_a / m_a + d_{wx} \\ \ddot{y}_a = (\cos\phi_a \sin\theta_a \sin\psi_a - \sin\phi_a \cos\psi_a)u_1 / m_a - k_y \dot{y}_a / m_a + d_{wy} \\ \ddot{z}_a = (\cos\phi_a \sin\theta_a)u_1 / m_a - g - k_z \dot{z}_a / m_a + d_{wz} \\ \ddot{\phi}_a = \dot{\theta}_a \dot{\psi}_a (I_y - I_z) / I_x - \dot{\theta}_a \Lambda I_r / I_x + u_2 / I_x - k_\phi \dot{\phi}_a / I_x + d_{w\phi} \\ \ddot{\theta} = \dot{\phi}_a \dot{\psi}_a (I_z - I_x) / I_y - \dot{\phi}_a \Lambda I_r / I_y + u_3 / I_y - k_\theta \dot{\theta}_a / I_y + d_{w\theta} \\ \ddot{\psi} = \dot{\phi}_a \dot{\theta}_a (I_x - I_y) / I_z + u_4 / I_z - k_\psi \dot{\psi}_a / I_z + d_{w\psi} \end{cases} \quad (1)$$

which $X_a = [x_a, y_a, z_a]^T$ represents the position information of the UAV in the geodetic coordinate system. $\omega = [\phi_a, \theta_a, \psi_a]^T$ represents the attitude information of the UAV. $V_a = [\dot{x}_a, \dot{y}_a, \dot{z}_a, \dot{\phi}_a, \dot{\theta}_a, \dot{\psi}_a]^T$ indicates the linear and angular velocities of the UAV along the x-axis, y-axis, and z-axis in its own coordinate system, u_1, u_2, u_3, u_4 indicate the four control inputs of the UAV. Ultimately, the mathematical model of a UAV can be expressed as:

$$\begin{cases} \dot{X}_a = V_a \\ \dot{V}_a = Au_a + f(X_a) + \Delta f(X_a) + d_{wi} \end{cases} \quad (2)$$

The USV dynamics model in the geodetic coordinate system [1]can be expressed as:

$$
\begin{cases}
\dot{x}_s = u_s \cos(\psi_s) - v_s \sin(\psi_s) \\
\dot{y}_s = u_s \sin(\psi_s) + v_s \cos(\psi_s) \\
\dot{\psi}_s = r_s \\
\dot{u}_s = f_u(\cdot) + (1/m_u)\tau_u + d_{wu}/m_u \\
\dot{v}_s = f_v(\cdot) + d_{wv}m_v \\
\dot{r}_s = f_r(\cdot) + \tau_r/m_r + d_{wrr}/m_r
\end{cases}
\tag{3}
$$

which $X_s = [x_s, y_s]^T$ indicates the position information of the USV in the geodetic coordinate system, ψ_s is yaw angle of the USV, $V_s = [u_s, v_s, r_s]^T$ represents the linear and angular velocities of the USV in its own coordinate system. τ_u, τ_r are control inputs for USVs. The model uncertainty term functions are $f_u(\cdot), f_v(\cdot), f_r(\cdot)$.

2.2 Description of the problems

Considering a heterogeneous system consisting of a single USV, a UAV is used as a leader, and the horizontal position information of the UAV is transmitted to the USV using the equivalent mapping technique, and the trajectory tracking control of the USV is carried out, so as to accomplish the cooperative control of sea and air. In order to realize the above control objectives, the following assumptions are made for the system: Assumption 1: The UAV attitude system is stable; Assumption 2: The position information of the UAV can be transmitted to the USV without delay in the transmission process; Assumption 3: The USV has sufficient control capability to achieve accurate tracking of the UAV trajectory; Assumption 4: The presence of model uncertainty in the UAV and USV is bounded and external perturbations are bounded; Assumption 5: The UAV desired trajectory and desired velocity are bounded.

2.3. System flow chart

The structure diagram of the fixed-time heterogeneous distribution strategy proposed in this paper is shown in Figure 1.

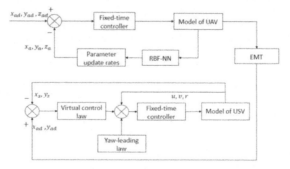

Figure 1. System flow chart

3 Fixed-time controller design

3.1 Design of fixed-time controller for UAV

Define a sliding mold surface of fixed time form as follows:

$$s_a = V_{ae} + g_1 Sig^{\gamma_1}(X_{ae}) + g_2 L_a^{\gamma_2}(X_{ae}) \tag{4}$$

which $g_1 = diag\{g_{11}, g_{12}, g_{13}\}$, $g_2 = diag\{g_{21}, g_{22}, g_{23}\}$ are coefficient diagonal matrix, γ_1, γ_2 fulfillment $\gamma_1 > 1, 0 < \gamma_2 < 1$. Then the control law of UAV can be derived from the inverse step and fixed time theory:

$$u_a = A^{-1}\left[-f(X_a) + \ddot{X}_{ad} - g_1\Theta_1 V_{ae} - g_2\Theta_2 V_{ae} - (k_a + \eta_1)\operatorname{sign}(s_a) - k_b s_a s_a^T s_a\right] \tag{5}$$

which k_a is a positive number to be designed, η_1 is an unknown bounded positive number. $k_b = diag\{k_x, k_y, k_z\}$ is a gain diagonal matrix.

3.2 Design of fixed-time controller for USV

For USV, the thrust actuators are configured only in the direction of the surge, so there can be $z_{se} = \sqrt{x_{se}^2 + y_{se}^2}$, and the virtual control law can be designed as the following equation:

$$\begin{cases} \alpha_u = \cos(\psi_{sv})^{-1}\left[\dot{x}_{sl}\cos(\psi_{sd}) + \dot{y}_{sl}\sin(\psi_{sd}) - v_s\sin(\psi_{se}) + k_1 sig^{\frac{1}{2}}(z_e - \eta_\Delta) + k_2 sig^{\frac{3}{2}}(z_e - \eta_\Delta)\right] \\ \alpha_r = k_3 sig^{\frac{1}{2}}(\psi_{se}) + k_4 sig^{\frac{3}{2}}(\psi_{se}) + \dot{\psi}_{sd} \end{cases} \tag{6}$$

3.3 Adaptive RBF-NN

Reasoning leads to the control law [3] design result for UAV-USV as:

$$\begin{cases} u_a = A^{-1}\left[-f(X_a) + \ddot{X}_{ad} - g_1\Theta_1 V_{ae} - g_2\Theta_2 V_{ae} - (k_a + \hat{\eta}_1)\operatorname{sign}(s_a) - k_b s_a s_a^T s_a\right] \\ \tau_u = \dot{\alpha}_u + m_u(z_e - \eta_\Delta)\cos(\psi_{se}) - k_{11}Sig^{\frac{1}{2}}(u_{se}) - k_{22}Sig^{\frac{3}{2}}(u_{se}) - \hat{\vartheta}_u - u_{se}\frac{\|S_u(\upsilon)\|^2}{\phi_{1u}}\hat{\varphi}_{su} \\ \tau_r = \dot{\alpha}_r - k_{33}sig^{\frac{1}{2}}(r_{se}) - k_{44}sig^{\frac{3}{2}}(r_{se}) - \dot{\psi}_{se} - \hat{\vartheta}_r - r_{se}\frac{\|S_r(\upsilon)\|^2}{\phi_{1r}}\hat{\varphi}_{sr} \end{cases} \tag{7}$$

4. Proof of stability

Proof: the Lyapunov function can be defined as:

$$V_a = \frac{1}{2}X_{ae}^T X_{ae} \tag{8}$$

The derivation of this gives:

$$\dot{V}_a = X_{ae}^T V_{ae} \leq -M_1 V_a^{\frac{\gamma_1+1}{2}} - M_2 V_a^{\frac{\gamma_2+1}{2}} \tag{9}$$

which $\gamma_1 > 1, 0 < \gamma_2 < 1, M_1 = \min\{2^{\frac{\gamma_1+1}{2}} g_{1i}\} > 0, M_2 = \min\{2^{\frac{\gamma_2+1}{2}} g_{2i}\} > 0$.

Consider the following Lyapunov candidate function:

$$V_s = \frac{1}{2}(z_e - \eta_\Delta)^2 + \frac{1}{2}\psi_{se}^2 + \frac{1}{2}m_u u_{se}^2 + \frac{1}{2}m_r r_{se}^2 \tag{10}$$

Derivation of this gives:

$$\dot{V}_s \leq -aV_s^{\frac{3}{4}} - bV_s^{\frac{5}{4}} + \Gamma \tag{11}$$

5. Numerical simulation

Numerical simulation is used to verify the effectiveness and stability of the designed fixed-time based cooperative control law for UAV and USV, which consists of a pilot UAV and a following USV. The reference trajectory of the UAV is $X_{ad} = [2\cos(0.5t),$ $2\sin(0.5t), 0.1t]^T$, the initial position of the drone is $X_{a0} = [1.9, 0, 0]^T$, the initial position of the USV is $X_{s0} = [-5, 0, 0]^T$, The following are the numerical simulation results:

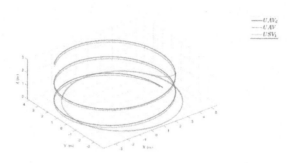

Figure. 2 Trajectory of UAV-USV in 3D coordinate system

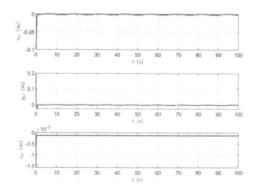

Figure. 3 Position and altitude tracking errors of the UAV

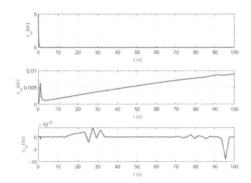

Figure. 4 Position and yaw angle error of the USV

Figure. 2 represents the trajectories of UAV and USV under external disturbances and parameter uncertainties. From the simulation results, it can be seen that both UAVs and USVs can track the desired trajectories well; Figure. 3 and 4 represent the position tracking errors of the UAVs and USVs, and it can be clearly seen that by using the proposed control law, the errors of trajectory tracking can be converged to the region close to zero in the presence of external disturbances, parametric disturbances, or other disturbances. In the presence of time-varying formations and disturbances, the controllers designed in this study are able to enable the UAVs and USVs with different initial states to complete the trajectory tracking control in a fixed period of time.

6. Conclusion

This paper investigates the cooperative control problem of UAV-USV system under model uncertainty and external perturbation. Firstly, based on the equivalent mapping technique, the motion trajectories of the UAV and the USV are linked, which solves the problem of model heterogeneity that does not facilitate the design of controllers. Secondly, based on the fixed-time theory and inverse-step method, the controllers of the USV are designed. And lastly, for the unknown term, RBF-NN is introduced and the minimum parameter method is used to update the individual scalars to simplify the parameter computation amount, and the fixed-time adaptive law. The simulation results show that the designed controller can make the UAV and the USV realize the control target in a certain time.

References

[1] Bai JQ, Wang YK, Xing H. Fixed-time heterogeneous formation control of unmanned boats and quadcopter unmanned aerial vehicles [J]. Systems engineering and electronic technology, 2023, 45(4):12. doi:10.12305/j.issn.1001-506X.2023.04.24.
[2] Wan L, Cao Y, Sun Y, et al. Fault-tolerant trajectory tracking control for unmanned surface vehicle with actuator faults based on a fast fixed-time system[J]. ISA transactions, 2022, 130:79-91. doi:10.1016/j.isatra.2022.04.013.
[3] Tian Y, Du C, Lu P, et al. Nonsingular fixed-time attitude coordinated tracking control for multiple rigid spacecraft[J]. ISA transactions, 2022, 129(Pt B):243-256. doi:10.1016/j. isatra. 2022.02.024.
[4] Du Z, Xue H, Ahn C K, et al. Event‐triggered adaptive tracking control for high‐order multi‐agent systems with unknown control directions[J]. International Journal of Robust and Nonlinear

Control, 2021, 31(18): 8937-8960. doi:10.1002/rnc.5768.

[5]   Yang R, Zhang H, Feng G, et al. Robust cooperative output regulation of multi-agent systems via adaptive event-triggered control[J]. Automatica, 2019, 102:129-136. doi: 10.1016/j.automatica.2019.01.001.

[6]   Shen Z, Wang Y, Yu H, et al. Finite-time adaptive tracking control of marine vehicles with complex unknowns and input saturation[J].Ocean Engineering, 2020, 198:106980. doi:10.1016/j.oceaneng.2020.106980.

Computer Systems and Communication Technology
W. Zheng (Ed.)
© 2024 The Authors.
doi:10.3233/ATDE240007

The Use of Python, Owlready, Sparql in Processing the Words Ontological Model of Public Political Discourse

Ayaulym SAIRANBEKOVA[a,1], Gulmira BEKMANOVA [b], Assel OMARBEKOVA [c],
Assel MUKANOVA [d] and Altanbek ZULKHAZHAV [e]

[a,b,c,e] *L. N. Gumilyov Eurasian National University*
[d] *Astana International University*

ORCiD ID: Ayaulym SAIRANBEKOVA https://orcid.org/0000-0002-0814-1532,
Gulmira BEKMANOVA https://orcid.org/0000-0001-8554-7627,
Assel OMARBEKOVA https://orcid.org/0000-0002-9272-8829,
Assel MUKANOVA https://orcid.org/0000-0002-8964-3891,
Altanbek ZULKHAZHAV https://orcid.org/0000-0002-4491-3253

Abstract. The article describes a technology processing ontological model of words in public political discourse. The research task is developing an information question-answering system of political discourse in Kazakh language. The Python programming language, Sparql data-query language, and Owlready module are used to develop the system.

Keywords. Artificial intelligence; knowledge base; discourse; ontology; formalization, python, owlready, sparql, OWL.

1. Introduction

This work is carried out within the framework of the project BR11765535 "Development of Scientific and Linguistic Foundations and IT Resources to Expand the Functions and Improve the Culture of the Kazakh Language".

The authors of the article are conducting work related to the processing of sentiment in socio-political discourse and public speeches [1], knowledge acquisition based on ontologies in natural language processing [2], and ontology process using python and sparql [3].

Nowadays, many people express their civic and political positions through the social networks.

The processors have already been made that work in this direction based on artificial intelligence methods. In Kazakhstan, scientists from L.N. Gumilyov Eurasian National University [4, 5], Al-Farabi Kazakh National University [6], and the International University of Information Technologies (International Information Technologies University) [7] researched the sentiment analyzer of official and unofficial information sources based on the texts sentiments analysis.

---

[1] Corresponding Author: Ayaulym Sairanbekova, sairanbekova98@gmail.com

An academic ontology is a specification of concepts, their attributes, and relationships in a certain subject area [1]. Ontologies allow to perform logical inference to get new information by reasoning and link it together with different pieces of knowledge from the ontology [8]. The Protégé editor is mainly used to create, maintain, and evaluate ontologies. However, it is not enough to develop the interface of its applications [9]. The data-query language SPARQL is mainly used for ontology programming interfaces; we used the OWLAPI module in our work.

The module was used for making a tool processing biomedical ontologies [10], a data system connecting different bulletin boards using an ontology coordination approach [11], explaining contingencies in production planning [12], a semantic web infrastructure analyzing dataflow [13,14].

2. Ontology Data Processing Algorithm

The question-and-answering system on public political discourse is available at the link https://kazlangres.enu.kz/#/answer/question/3.

This system was developed based on the ontology of political discourse (https://webprotege.stanford.edu/#projects/16410306-5223-4a1b-85bf-61fb3bd3a5e1/edit/Classes?selection=Class(owl:Thing)).

System operation algorithm:
1. database of questions is formed on ontology base,
2. all questions are stored in the database,
3. all answers to generated questions are stored in the database,
4. user asks a question,
5. the question text is being checked for the presence of an entity,
6. if the question matches a keyword in the ontology, then all answers associated with this entity are returned.
7. if the question does not match the keyword in the ontology, the question is checked with the generated questions,
8. if the question matches the generated questions, then all similar questions and their answers are returned.

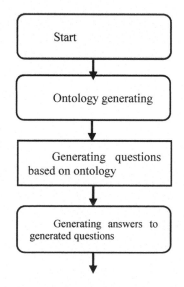

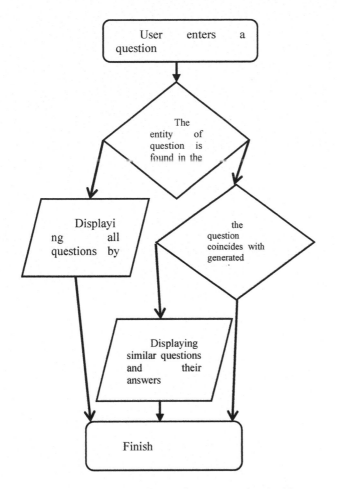

Figure 1. System operation algorithm.

The procedures are described below.

The procedure for generating questions based on ontology:
questions = [
# Дегеніміз не деген сұрақтар формасы
{
    'question': random.choice(["{} дегеніміз не?#0", "{} деген не?#0"]),
    'query': '''
        SELECT ?olabel ?label
            WHERE { ?subject rdfs:subClassOf ?object .
        ?subject rdfs:label ?label .
        ?object rdfs:label ?olabel
        FILTER(
            (REGEX(STR(?label), "'' + question.lower() + '''') || REGEX(STR(?label),
'''' + question + '''') || REGEX(STR(?label), '' + question.capitalize() + ''''))
)

```
        }
        order by   ?label
    ''',
    'answer': "{} дегеніміз - {}#0",
},


{
    'question':  random.choice([source  +"  бойынша  {}  анықтамасы#2",  "{}
анықтамасы#2", "{} анықтамасын айт#2"]),
    'query': '''
      SELECT ?object ?label
         WHERE { ?subject kazont:definition ?object .
      ?subject rdfs:label ?label .
      FILTER(
         (REGEX(STR(?label), "'" + question.lower() + "'") || REGEX(STR(?label),
"'" + question + "'") || REGEX(STR(?label) ,"' + question.capitalize() + "'"))
         )


      }
    ''',
    'answer': random.choice(["{} анықтамасы: {}#2", "{} дегеніміз: {}#0"]),
},
{
    'question': random.choice(["{} үшін мысал келтір#2", source + " бойынша {}
үшін қандай мысалдар келтірілген#2", "{} мысалдары#2"]),
    'query': '''
      SELECT ?subject ?label
      WHERE
      {
        {
        ?subject rdf:type ?object .
        ?object rdfs:label ?label .
        FILTER(
        (REGEX(STR(?label) ,"'" + question + "'") || REGEX(STR(?label), "' +
question.capitalize() + "'"))
           && (LANG(?label) = "" || LANG(?label) = "kz" )
           )
        }
        union
        {
        ?object kazont:example ?subject .
        ?object rdfs:label ?label .
        FILTER(
        (REGEX(STR(?label), "'" + question + "'") || REGEX(STR(?label), "' +
question.capitalize() + "'"))
           && (LANG(?label) = "" || LANG(?label) = "kz" )
           )


        }
```

```
        }
    ''',
    'answer': random.choice(["{} үшін мысалдар: {}#0", "{} мысалдары: {}#2"]),

},

{
    'question': random.choice(["{} түрлері қандай?#2", "{} " + source + "
бойынша қандай түрлерге бөлінеді#0"]),
    'query': '''
        SELECT ?slabel ?label
            WHERE { ?subject rdfs:subClassOf ?object .
        ?object rdfs:label ?label .
        ?subject rdfs:label ?slabel .
        FILTER((REGEX(STR(?label), "" + question + "") || REGEX(STR(?label), "
+ question.capitalize() + "")) && (LANG(?slabel) = "" || LANG(?slabel) = "kz" ) )
        }
    ''',
    'answer': random.choice(["{} түрлері: {}#2", "{} келесідей бөлінеді: {}#0"]),
}

]
```

Question update procedure:

```
def update_question(self, question):
    try:
        # Database Connection
        if self.cursor.closed:
            self._delete_instance()
            self = self.get_instance()
        cursor = self.cursor
        # Checking if a question exists in the database
        cursor.execute("SELECT id FROM public.question WHERE question = %s",
(question['question'],))
        question_id = cursor.fetchone()

        if not question_id:
            # If there is no question, insert it into the 'question' table
            print(cursor.execute("INSERT INTO public.question (question) VALUES
(%s) RETURNING id", (question['question'],)))
            question_id = cursor.fetchone()['id']

        # Inserting question-related answers into the 'answer' table         for
answer_data in question['answers']:
            cursor.execute("INSERT    INTO    public.answer    (answer,    question_id)
VALUES (%s, %s)", (answer_data['answer'], question_id))

        # Save change
        self.connection.commit()
        # Closing cursor
```

```
        cursor.close()
        return True  # Inserted successfully
    except Exception as e:
        print(f" Error inserting into database: {str(e)}")
        self.connection.rollback()    # Transaction rollback in case of error
return False  # An error occurred while inserting
```

`pg_trgm` for postgresql is used for searching questions from the database. `pg_trgm` is an extension to PostgreSQL providing support for operators and functions for performing operations on the lines using trigrams. Trigrams are groups of three sequential character in a line. This extension provides powerful tools for performing various operations with the text, such as detecting similar lines, performing similar trigram counting, and much more.

Some of the key functions and operators provided by `pg_trgm` are:

1. **similarity(text1 text, text2 text)**: This function compares two texts and returns similarity value between them. It uses trigrams to calculate similarity, and the result is represented as a floating-point number ranging from 0 to 1, where 0 indicates no similarity at all and 1 indicates a complete match.

2. **"%" и "<%"**: These operators can be used to perform comparisons of text lines using trigrams. "%" returns "true" if two lines have similarity more than 0.3, while `<%` returns `true' if the similarity is more than 0.6.

3. **word_similarity(text1 text, text2 text)**: This function works similar to `similarity()`, but it only considers words, not characters.

4. **show_trgm(text text)**: This function returns an array of trigrams for the specified text.

Using "pg_trgm" can be useful for implementing full-text search, as well as for searching for similar texts and auto-completion of text queries. It carries efficient searching even in the cases where texts can contain typos or spelling variations.

```
    def get_question_similarity(self, question):
        try:
            # Database Connection
            if self.cursor.closed:
                self._delete_instance()
                self = self.get_instance()
            cursor = self.cursor

            # Request to get a question by its ID
            cursor.execute('''
            SELECT id, question FROM
                (SELECT id, question, similarity(question, %s) AS sim
            FROM
                question
            WHERE
                similarity(question, %s) > 0.3) AS quest
            ORDER BY
                sim DESC
            LIMIT 10''', (question,question))
            question_datas = cursor.fetchall()
            result = []
```

```
    for question_data in question_datas:
        question_id = question_data['id']
    # Runnnig a query to get answers related to the question
cursor.execute("SELECT * FROM public.answer WHERE question_id = %s",
(question_id,))
        answers_data = cursor.fetchall()

    # Dictionary formation based on the received data        question_dict
= {
            'question': question_data['question'],
            'answers':  [{'answer':  answer_data['answer']}   for   answer_data   in
answers_data]
        }
        result.append(question_dict)

     # Closing cursor
        cursor.close()
        return result
    except Exception as e:
        print(f" Error while retrieving data from database:
{str(e)}")
        return None
```

If a question is not found in the question database, then the search procedure for a similar question is performed (a function for calculating the Levenshtein distance between two lines):   levenshteinDistance(a, b) {

```
    if (a.length === 0) return b.length;
    if (b.length === 0) return a.length;

    const matrix = [];

    // Fill in the matrix
    for (let i = 0; i <= b.length; i++) {
      matrix[i] = [i];
    }

    for (let j = 0; j <= a.length; j++) {
      matrix[0][j] = j;
    }

    for (let i = 1; i <= b.length; i++) {
      for (let j = 1; j <= a.length; j++) {
        const cost = a.charAt(j - 1) === b.charAt(i - 1) ? 0 : 1;
        matrix[i][j] = Math.min(
          matrix[i - 1][j] + 1,
          matrix[i][j - 1] + 1,
          matrix[i - 1][j - 1] + cost
        );
      }
    }
```

```
    }

    return matrix[b.length][a.length];
  },
this.questions.sort((a,b)=>
      this.levenshteinDistance(a.question,          this.question)          -
this.levenshteinDistance(b.question, this.question)
     );
```

3. Conclusion

The practical significance of the study is focus on solving the applied problem of developing a question-answering system based on the ontology of political discourse. The operation algorithm of the question-answering system, the knowledge base formation of questions and answers based on the knowledge base are described, and the Python program codes for system use are described in detail. The obtain results can certainly be applied developing applications in various subject areas basing on ontologies.

Summing up, we can draw conclusions about the relevance and development trends of this direction. To date, a lot of work is being done around the world in the direction of artificial intelligence and intelligent systems based on knowledge. The research carried out in this work gives new ideas and opens up new possibilities of intelligent systems based on bases of the knowledge for further work and study.

References

[1]   G. Bekmanova, B. Yergesh, A. Ukenova, A. Omarbekova, A. Mukanova, Y. Ongarbayev. Sentiment Processing of Socio-political Discourse and Public Speeches. Lecture Notes in Computer Science. Том 14108, pp. 191 – 205, ICCSA 2023, doi:10.1007/978-3-031-37117-2_15

[2]   G.Yelibayeva, A. Sharipbay, G. Bekmanova, A. Omarbekova. Ontology-based extraction of Kazakh language word combinations in natural language processing. ACM International Conference Proceeding Series. pp. 58 - 595, DATA 2021. doi:10.1145/3460620.3460631.

[3]   A. Omarbekova, A. Sharipbay, A. Barlybaev. Generation of Test Questions from RDF Files Using PYTHON and SPARQL. Journal of Physics: Conference Series. Том 806, Выпуск 121, CCEAI 2017. doi: 10.1088/1742-6596/806/1/012009.

[4]   B. Yergesh, L. Kenzhina. Analysis of the users' emotional state in social networks. ACM International Conference Proceeding Series. Article number 3492654. 7th International Conference on Engineering and MIS, ICEMIS 2021. 2021. Код 175544. ISBN 978-145039044-6. doi: 10.1145/3492547.3492654.

[5]   A. Boranbayev, G. Shuitenov, S. Boranbayev. The Method of Analysis of Data from Social Networks Using Rapidminer. Advances in Intelligent Systems and Computing. Volume 1229 AISC, Pp. 667 – 673. 2020 Science and Information Conference, 2020. Код 241959. ISSN 21945357. ISBN 978-303052245-2. doi: 10.1007/978-3-030-52246-9_49.

[6]   D. Sultan, A. Suliman, A. Toktarova, B. Omarov, S. Mamikov, G. Beissenova. Cyberbullying detection and prevention: Data mining in social media. Proceedings of the Confluence 2021: 11th International Conference on Cloud Computing, Data Science and Engineering. Pp.338 – 342. Article number 9377077 11th International Conference on Cloud Computing, Data Science and Engineering, Confluence. 2021. Код 167955. ISBN 978-073813160-3. doi:10.1109/Confluence51648.2021.9377077.

[7]   B. Gulnara, Z. Ilyas, Z. Gulnara. The development of a web application for the automatic analysis of the tonality of texts based on machine learning methods. International Conference on Control, Automation and Systems. Volume 2018. Article number 8571950. 18th International Conference on Control, Automation and Systems, ICCAS 2018. Код 143670. ISSN 15987833. ISBN 978-899321515-1.

[8] N. Guarino, D. Oberle, S. Staab, Handbook on ontologies, Springer, 2009, Ch. What Is an Ontology?, pp. 1–17.

[9] A. Rector, M. Horridge, L. Iannone, N. Drummond, Use Cases for Building OWL Ontologies as Modules: Localizing, Ontology and Programming Interfaces & Extensions, in: 4th Int Workshop on Semantic Web enabled software engineering (SWESE-08), 2008.

[10] J.-B. Lamy, Owlready: Ontology-oriented programming in Python with automatic classification and high level constructs for biomedical ontologies. Artificial Intelligence in Medicine. Vol. 80, pp. 11 – 28. 2017. doi: 10.1016/j.artmed.2017.07.002.

[11] R. Jain, N. Duhan. OntoJob Query Processor: An Ontology Driven Query Processing Method in Jobology Information System. Journal of Computer Science. Vol. 16, Выпуск 5, pp. 702 – 714. 2020. doi: 10.3844/JCSSP.2020.702.714.

[12] P. Schuller. A new OWLAPI interface for HEX-programs applied to explaining contingencies in production planning. CEUR Workshop Proceedings. Vol. 2659, pp. 25 – 31. 2020. NeHuAI 2020.

[13] E. Jajaga, L. Ahmedi. C-SWRL: A Unique Semantic Web Framework for Reasoning over Stream Data. International Journal of Semantic Computing. Vol. 11, Выпуск 3, pp. 391 – 409. 2017. doi: 10.1142/S1793351X17400165.

[14] E. Jajaga, L. Ahmedi. C-SWRL: A Unique Semantic Web Framework for Reasoning over Stream Data. International Journal of Semantic Computing. Vol. 11, Выпуск 3, pp. 391 – 409. 2017. DOI 10.1142/S1793351X17400165] [E. Jajaga, L. Ahmedi. C-SWRL: SWRL for Reasoning over Stream Data. ICSC 2017. Pp. 395 – 400. doi: 10.1109/ICSC.2017.64

54

Computer Systems and Communication Technology
W. Zheng (Ed.)
© 2024 The Authors.
This article is published online with Open Access by IOS Press and distributed under the terms
of the Creative Commons Attribution Non-Commercial License 4.0 (CC BY-NC 4.0).
doi:10.3233/ATDE240008

Driving Behavior Correlation Analysis Method Based on Apriori Algorithm

TIANJUN SUN[a,b,c], HONGYU HU[a,b,c,1], JUNJIE WU[c] and ZHENGCAI YANG[d]

[a] *Changsha Automobile Innovation Research Institute, Jilin University, Changsha 410016, China*
[b] *State Key Laboratory of Automotive Simulation and Control, Jilin University, Changchun 130022, China*
[c] *College of Automotive Engineering, Jilin University, Changchun 130022, China*
[d] *Key Laboratory of Automotive Power Train and Electronics, Hubei University of Automotive Technology, Shiyan 442000,China*
ORCiD ID: TIANJUN SUN https://orcid.org/0000-0002-7627-8151

Abstract. The purpose of this paper is to investigate the interactions between driver manipulation behaviors. Firstly, representative samples from driving behavior dataset were screened. Secondly, four characteristic indicators were constructed. Thirdly, the Apriori algorithm was established for correlation analysis on these four driving behaviors in order to obtain the influence relationship between different driving behaviors. Therefore, the correlation between different undesirable driving behaviors and reveals the intrinsic law of driver manipulation behavior were illustrated, which provided great significance for improving the warning effect and intervention efficiency of automotive active safety systems.

Keywords. Driving behavior, correlation analysis, traffic safety, apriori algorithm

1. Introduction

With the development of the economy and improvement of living standards, the number of vehicles is increasing exponentially, and the scale of road traffic is gradually diversifying and quantifying[1]. As the decision maker and controller of the vehicle, the driver's judgments and behavioral choices will have an important impact on the road traffic closed-loop system. Therefore, it is of great significance to carry out in-depth elaboration and correlation analysis of drivers' adverse behaviors, scientifically and reasonably describe driving behaviors, and reveal the complex correlation between adverse driving behaviors, which can provide a theoretical basis for the prevention and reduction of road traffic accidents[2–4].

This paragraph reviews some methods and applications of driving behavior data mining from different literature sources. Literature[5] used statistical machine learning techniques to model, predict, and detect driver behavior and risk based on data from actual driving scenarios. Literature[6] ranked the importance of accident causes using AHP hierarchical analysis and analyzed the degree and level of influence of accidents using Apriori algorithm. Literature[7] proposed a novel model for identifying driver

---

[1] Corresponding Author: HONGYU HU, huhongyu@jlu.edu.cn

behavior based on trajectory data that can protect the privacy of driver trajectories. It used a joint clustering method with local Bayesian-Gaussian mixture and global K-means algorithms.

In summary, there is less existing research on driver behavioral characteristics and the correlations between them. Since driving behaviors are interrelated in the driving process, and most traffic accidents are not caused by a single adverse driving behavior, analyzing the correlation of driving behaviors can provide more comprehensive guidance for the design of road traffic safety systems. In this paper, we proposed a method based on the Apriori algorithm to mine the association rules between adverse driving behaviors in a driver, which can provide more comprehensive guidance for the design of road traffic safety systems.

2. Driving behavior evaluation model based on threshold method

The goal of this study is to investigate the connection between driving behavior data. Vehicle motion reflects driver operations and can be used to evaluate driving behavior. Speed and acceleration are key parameters demonstrating vehicle motion and related to driver control over the vehicle's longitudinal direction. This paper selects speed and acceleration data from BDD100K dataset[8] as research object and builds a driving behavior evaluation model based on speed and acceleration parameters using actual driving data, and conducts correlation analysis of different types of bad driving behavior according to this model. The map of BDD100K dataset collection locations is as shown in **Figure 1**.

Figure 1. Map of BDD100K dataset collection locations.

2.1. Average speeding behavior

Speeding behavior is one of the main causes of traffic accidents, which not only increases the probability of accidents but also aggravates their severity. This article uses average speed to measure acceleration behavior, reflecting the driver's tendency and risk level. The maximum speed limit of urban roads is generally 50km/h, but in practice it will be affected by traffic conditions, and drivers cannot keep the maximum speed all the time. Therefore, when calculating the average speed over the speed limit, the maximum speed limit cannot simply be used as the threshold, and a lower threshold should be selected. In this paper, the quartile difference method is used to determine the average speed exceeding threshold, and a reasonable threshold range is obtained, and the calculation of the quartile difference method is shown in Eq. (1):

$$V_{mean} = Q + 1.5I \tag{1}$$

Where V_{mean} denotes the average speed exceeding threshold, Q represents the 75th percentile of all average speed samples in the dataset, and I denote the interquartile difference of the average speed sample. According to the calculations, the average speed exceeding the threshold is 37.6km/h, and beyond this, the driving behavior is regarded as bad driving behavior and assigned a value of 1 during data discretization.

2.2. Rapid speed change behavior

Rapid speed change behavior is a common bad driving behavior that not only affects occupant comfort, but also affects vehicle performance. Rapid speed change reflects the driver's inexperience or nervousness, and the behavior reduces driving safety and efficiency. Therefore, it is necessary to consider the indicators of rapid acceleration and deceleration behavior in the driving behavior evaluation model. In this paper, the maximum change value of acceleration during the trip is adopted as the evaluation index of rapid acceleration and deceleration behavior, and the larger the value is, the more aggressive the driver's driving behavior is, and the more likely to cause undesirable consequences. The acceleration fluctuation value is calculated as shown in Eq. (2):

$$a_f = a_+ + |a_-| \tag{2}$$

Where a_f indicates the fluctuation value of acceleration in the driving record, a_+ is the maximum value of acceleration in the driving data record, and a_- is the maximum value of deceleration in the driving data record. Combined with other references on the definition of the rapid speed change behavior and in the urban working conditions of the acceleration change rule of consideration, this paper will be the rapid speed change behavior threshold is determined as 2.2m/s^2. when the acceleration change value exceeds this threshold is considered to be the driving behavior there is a rapid speed change behavior, and for the discretization of the data after the assignment of the value of 1.

2.3. Large speed fluctuation behavior

Vehicle speed fluctuation behavior refers to the phenomenon of constant changes in vehicle driving speed due to the driver's operation of the brake pedal and gas pedal, or changes in the road environment during the driving process. When there is excessive speed fluctuation, it not only leads to instability in the traffic flow, but also increases the risk of collision between vehicles and the need for braking. Therefore, it is necessary to consider the speed fluctuation index in the driving behavior evaluation model. In the speed fluctuation analysis, the maximum speed and average speed of a trip should be determined first, then the difference between the maximum speed and average speed is the speed fluctuation, as shown in Eq. (3):

$$V_d = V_{max} - V_{mean} \tag{3}$$

In the formula, V_d indicates the size of speed fluctuation, V_{max} indicates the maximum speed, and V_{mean} indicates the average speed Combined with the speed fluctuation threshold selected in other references and the empirical law of speed fluctuation under urban road conditions, this paper selects the speed fluctuation threshold of 17km/h. Exceeding this threshold is regarded as speed fluctuation in the driving process, and the discretized data matrix is assigned a value of 1.

2.4. Frequent speed change behavior

Frequent speed change behavior refers to the driver's continuous acceleration or continuous braking within a certain period of time, resulting in constant changes in vehicle speed. This behavior will lead to distraction of the driver's attention, narrowing of the field of vision, prolonged reaction time, and decreased judgment ability, thus increasing the risk of traffic accidents. Therefore, it is necessary to consider frequent shifting indicators in the driving behavior evaluation model. Combining the speed fluctuation thresholds selected from other references and the empirical laws on vehicle speed change under urban road conditions, speed change greater than $1m/s^2$ is defined as one speed change, and the number of speed changes per unit time is defined as the speed change frequency, as shown in Eq. (4):

$$freq = A / t \tag{4}$$

Where *freq* is the frequency of speed change, A is the number of speed changes, and t is the unit time. When the value of *freq* is greater than 1 cpm, the driving process is defined as frequent speed change, which is considered to be a bad driving behavior, and the value of 1 is assigned to the discretized data matrix.

3. Driving behavior association rule analysis based on Apriori algorithm

The correlation analysis of driving behavior based on Apriori algorithm is a method based on the principle of frequent item set mining, which reveals the internal logic and influencing factors of driving behavior by discovering frequent patterns between different data. In this chapter, the Apriori algorithm is used to analyze the correlation of driving behavior characteristics screened in previous chapters.

3.1. Basic Concepts of Apriori Algorithm

Suppose there are two itemsets A, B. The core idea of Apriori algorithm is to predict the association rules of the data with the a priori knowledge, and measure the association between the data by calculating the support, confidence and lift. The support is a measure of the importance of the association rules, and the support is calculated as Eq. (5):

$$Support(A, B) = P(A \cup B) = \frac{NUM(A \cup B)}{NUM(ALL)} \tag{5}$$

Confidence is a measure of the accuracy of the association rules, confidence is calculated as in Eq. (6):

$$Confidence(A \rightarrow B) = P(B \mid A) = \frac{P(A \cup B)}{P(A)} = \frac{NUM(A \cup B)}{NUM(A)} \qquad (6)$$

Lift degree is used to indicate the degree of relevance of the two item sets, elevation degree of the formula as in Eq. (7):

$$Lift(A \rightarrow B) = \frac{P(B \mid A)}{P(B)} = \frac{P(A \cup B)}{P(A) \times P(B)} = \frac{NUM(A \cup B) \times NUM(ALL)}{NUM(A) \times NUM(B)} \qquad (7)$$

The flowchart of the Apriori algorithm is shown in **Figure 2**.

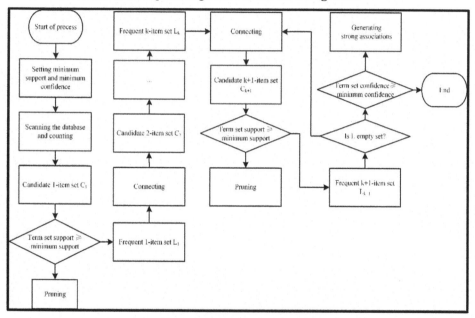

Figure 2. The flowchart of the Apriori algorithm.

3.2. Driving behavior correlation analysis

To facilitate the list, the four driving behavior features are numbered: average speed over-speed behavior is A, rapid speed change behavior is B, large speed fluctuation behavior is C, and frequent speed change behavior is D. Based on references[9,10] and engineering experience, this paper sets the minimum support degree to be 5% for all of them, and the minimum confidence level to be 20%. Scan the 42516 data files after preprocessing, count the number of occurrences of the four driving behavior features, and generate four candidate 1-item sets. The support of the four candidate 1-item sets is calculated, and all four are greater than the minimum support of 5%, so they are all retained to generate four frequent 1-item sets. **Table 1.** shows the four frequent 1-item sets and their support.

Table 1. Frequent 1-item sets of driving behavior characteristics

Frequent 1-item set	Support of set	Frequent 1-item set	Support of set	Frequent 1-item set	Support of set	Frequent 1-item set	Support of set
A	21.62%	B	17.62%	C	28.16%	D	32.73%

As shown in Table 2, the differences in the probability of occurrence of the four bad driving behaviors are relatively small, and all of them are more than all exceed the minimum support of 5%, so it is necessary to analyze them.

Six candidate 2-item sets are obtained after the joining operation of the frequent 1-item sets, and similarly, their support degrees are compared with the minimum support degree of 0.05, and three frequent 2-item sets that satisfy the minimum support degree requirement are obtained after the pruning step, and the support degree of the frequent 2-item sets reflects the probability of the two driving behavioral features occurring at the same time in a driving trip. **Table 2.** shows the three frequent 2-item sets and their support degrees.

Table 2. Frequent 2-item sets of driving behavior characteristics

Frequent 1-item set	Support of set	Frequent 1-item set	Support of set	Frequent 1-item set	Support of set
A → D	6.18%	B → D	6.31%	C → D	11.10%

By the same method, the candidate 3-item set is obtained from the frequent 2-item set, and after the pruning process, the frequent 3-item set is an empty set, so there is no case of three bad driving behaviors occurring at the same time in any driving trip in the driving dataset. Therefore, four frequent 1-item sets and three frequent 2-item sets are finally obtained, and the process of building driving behavior association rules is started. Through the screening above, three frequent 2-item sets were selected, and six association rules can be generated based on these three frequent 2-item sets depending on the antecedents. **Table 3.** gives the support, confidence and boosting of each association rule.

Table 3. Driving behavior association rule parameter table

Rule	Support	Confidence	Lift	Rule	Support	Confidence	Lift
A → D	6.18%	28.57%	0.873	D → B	6.31%	35.84%	1.095
D → A	6.18%	18.87%	0.873	C → D	11.10%	33.91%	1.206
B → D	6.31%	19.29%	1.095	D → C	11.10%	39.47%	1.206

Combining **Table 3.** and the initialized minimum confidence thresholds, three strongly correlated rules can be obtained as rules 4, 5, and 6. The analysis of these three strongly correlated rules is as follows.

For Rule 4, drivers who frequently shift gears tend to be aggressive and like to follow closely, overtake, and change lanes. They also like to press the pedal deeper for faster response and switch between the accelerator/brake pedals often. Therefore, frequent shifting behaviors are likely to co-occur with sharp shifting behaviors, and they increase the probability of sharp shifting behaviors happening. For Rule 5, the two bad driving behaviors of large speed fluctuation and frequent speed change are both affected by the urban road environment and driver psychology. They also have a positive feedback mechanism that makes them worsen each other. Thus, frequent speed change behaviors are likely to co-occur with large speed fluctuation behaviors, and they increase the probability of large speed fluctuation behaviors happening. For Rule 6, as described in Rule 5, there is a positive feedback mechanism between these two bad driving behaviors, which affect and worsen each other. As a result, frequent shifting behaviors are likely to co-occur with large speed fluctuation behaviors, and they increase the probability of large speed fluctuation behaviors happening.

4. Conclusion

This study analyzes the correlation of driving behavior features based on the Apriori algorithm, aiming to provide a basis for the design of automotive active safety systems and a theoretical foundation for the prevention and reduction of road traffic accidents. In this paper, firstly, based on the threshold method, four driving behavior features that can reflect drivers' bad behaviors are extracted from the BDD100K dataset; then, the correlation between the four driving behavior features is analyzed based on the Apriori algorithm. Finally, three strong association rules are mined, and there are high positive correlation and causal relationship between two driving behaviors.

5. Funding

This work was funded by the Innovation Project of Changsha Automotive Innovation Research Institute under Grant 20220106 and Key Laboratory of Automotive Power Train and Electronics of Hubei Province open fund project under Grant ZDK1202305.

References

[1]   Yuksel AS, Atmaca S. Driver's black box: a system for driver risk assessment using machine learning and fuzzy logic. Journal of intelligent transportation systems. 2021;25(5):482–500. doi:10.1080/15472450.2020.1852083

[2]   Lima AA, Das SC, Shahiduzzaman M. Driver Behavior Analysis Based on Numerical Data Using Deep Neural Networks. In: Lecture Notes in Networks and Systems [Internet]. 2022 [cited 2023 Aug 25]. p. 211–9. doi:10.1007/978-981-16-5348-3_16

[3]   Kumar R, Jain A. Driving behavior analysis and classification by vehicle OBD data using machine learning. J Supercomput [Internet]. 2023 May 19 [cited 2023 Aug 25] doi:10.1007/s11227-023-05364-3

[4]   Mozaffari S, Al-Jarrah OY, Dianati M, Jennings P, Mouzakitis A. Deep Learning-Based Vehicle Behavior Prediction for Autonomous Driving Applications: A Review. IEEE transactions on intelligent transportation systems. 2022;23(1):33–47. doi:10.1109/TITS.2020.3012034

[5]   Miyajima C, Takeda K. Driver-Behavior Modeling Using On-Road Driving Data: A new application for behavior signal processing. IEEE signal processing magazine. 2016;33(6):14–21. doi:10.1109/MSP.2016.2602377

[6]   Xi J, Zhao Z, Li W, Wang Q. A Traffic Accident Causation Analysis Method Based on AHP-Apriori. GREEN INTELLIGENT TRANSPORTATION SYSTEM AND SAFETY [Internet]. Amsterdam: Elsevier Science Bv; 2016 [cited 2023 Aug 25]. p. 680–687. (Procedia Engineering; vol. 138). doi:10.1016/j.proeng.2016.01.305

[7]   Lu L, Lin Y, Wen Y, Zhu J, Xiong S. Federated clustering for recognizing driving styles from private trajectories. Engineering applications of artificial intelligence. 2023;118(Journal Article):105714. doi:10.1016/j.engappai.2022.105714

[8]   Xu H, Gao Y, Yu F, Darrell T. End-to-end Learning of Driving Models from Large-scale Video Datasets. In: 30TH IEEE CONFERENCE ON COMPUTER VISION AND PATTERN RECOGNITION (CVPR 2017) [Internet]. New York: IEEE; 2017 [cited 2023 Aug 25]. p. 3530–8. doi:10.1109/CVPR.2017.376

[9]   Xie DF, Wang MH, Zhao XM. A Spatiotemporal Apriori Approach to Capture Dynamic Associations of Regional Traffic Congestion. IEEE Access. 2020;8:3695–709. doi:10.1109/ACCESS.2019.2962619

[10]   Hong J, Tamakloe R, Park D. Discovering Insightful Rules among Truck Crash Characteristics using Apriori Algorithm. J Adv Transp. 2020 Jan 16;2020:4323816. doi:10.1155/2020/432381

Computer Systems and Communication Technology
W. Zheng (Ed.)
© 2024 The Authors.
This article is published online with Open Access by IOS Press and distributed under the terms
of the Creative Commons Attribution Non-Commercial License 4.0 (CC BY-NC 4.0).
doi:10.3233/ATDE240009

Development of 3D Visualization Training System for Switch Room Safety Procedures

Qiu Wenjun[a], Guo Lai jia[b], Zhou Hong[b], Xu Shuai[b], Li Chao[a], Xiaojun Shen[c1]

[a] *Shanghai Minghua Electric Power Technology Co., LTD., Shanghai, 200090*
[b] *Shanghai Caojing Thermal Power Co., LTD., Shanghai, 201507*
[c] *Department of Electrical Engneering Tongji University, Shanghai 201804*
ORCiD ID: Xiaojun Shen https://orcid.org/0000-0002-5971-1259

Abstract. Safety procedures are the fundamental criteria to ensure the safety of personnel and equipment, and their proficiency and the rigor of the application are crucial. According to the actual existing training technology digital means is relatively backward, intuitive, affect the lack of training depth and effect, this paper to the switch room equipment as the object, based on 3Dmodeling and virtual simulation technology design and developed a can realize safety procedures learning, training of 3D visualization software tools, to solve the difficulty of maintenance training, safety procedures training tools missing problems.

Keywords. Switch room, 3D visualization, training, safety procedures

1. Introduction

The operation training and maintenance of operation personnel are the key to ensure the safety, stability and economic operation of equipment. In recent years, the repeated power plant safety accidents have exposed the personnel safety awareness is not in place, safety procedures do not master the major problems. The medium voltage switchgear cabinet in the switch room has high integration, including primary bus, switch, switch and complete secondary system, etc. Its operation and maintenance work requires special training. The medium voltage switchgear cannot be disassembled and trained during operation, which makes it difficult to quickly accumulate the front-line training experience of maintenance personnel. Even In the training environment, the medium voltage equipment in operation has the risk of electric shock and mechanical injury, resulting in the problems of difficult training of operation and maintenance personnel, high training time and economic cost. The safety procedures of personnel lack assessment tools, and it is difficult to truly measure the degree of personnel safety procedures only by passing the answer examination.

The development of 3Dmodeling and 3Dengine technology provides a feasible way to solve the above problems. By constructing high reduction degree switchgear digital operation scenario, developing advanced application for power plant operation and maintenance requirements, creating "simulated cockpit" for real scene, we can reduce

---

[1] Corresponding Author: Xiaojun Shen, xjshen79@163.com

training time cost, economic cost and opportunity cost, improve training quality and convenience, and have sufficient opportunity to be familiar with the process and content of the medium voltage switch gear, and no safety risk. Operation and maintenance personnel can operate freely, fully trial and error, different concerns about equipment failure shutdown or casualties. Through reasonable setting feedback mechanism, in a large number of trial and error, the operation and maintenance personnel are familiar with the dangerous points, which can quickly improve the safety awareness and dangerous operation awareness. When the open world switchgear operation and maintenance scenario is constructed, the simulation function of the operation and maintenance work applied in training has great value potential for mining. For example, safety awareness, safety skills, safety operation 3Drecord and assessment.

To sum up, taking the medium voltage switch room as an example, a set of digital 3Dscenario advanced application tools for power plant operation and maintenance needs have been developed to improve the training efficiency, reduce the training costs, eliminate the risk of trial and error, and improve the safety of power plant operation and maintenance and the reliability of equipment operation.

2. Training requirements analysis

At present, virtual reality technology is widely used in various fields, such as electronics, mechanical design, education, military and other [1-3]. Through the virtual reality technology, the equipment and scenes encountered in the operation and inspection work are faithfully restored, and the complex, abstract and two-dimensional data and information can be reflected in three-dimensional, intuitive and interactive ways, which is very suitable for the application and power training field [4,5]. Relying on the real three-dimensional model of power operation and maintenance scene and based on the constructed virtual reality environment, it can greatly improve the authenticity, immersion and interactivity of the power operation and maintenance scene system scene, which plays an important role in promoting the simulation and training working mode of power operation and maintenance scene personnel. [6-8]. Therefore, the power training requirements for 3Dvisualization should include the following parts:

Provides a "familiar" environment. By building a high reduction degree of switch room digital operations scenario, the development of advanced application for power plant operations demand, create the power plant people own "simulation cockpit", can reduce the plant training time cost, economic cost, opportunity cost, and improve the training quality and convenience, can make the operations personnel in the core equipment, can also have enough opportunity to be familiar with the medium voltage switch cabinet, familiar with the maintenance work process and content;

Avoid the cost of "trial and error". In the 3Ddigital training environment, the real simulation of the operating state of the switch room, and no security risk. Operation and maintenance personnel can operate freely, fully trial and error, different concerns about equipment failure shutdown or casualties. Through the reasonable setting of the feedback mechanism, in a large number of trial and error, is the operation and maintenance personnel familiar with the dangerous point, can quickly improve the safety awareness, dangerous operation alert awareness;

Eliminate the "empirical" risk. When the open world-type switchgear operation and maintenance scenario is built, the simulation functions applied to the operation and maintenance of the training still have great value potential to be explored. For example, it can realize 3Ddigital assessment, objective and fair record security practice.

3. Safety procedures: 3Dvisualization training system design

The general goal of the training system is to construct a 3-dimensional visual switch room environment, with safety regulations training and complete various training tasks; including field equipment cognition, environment cognition, safety knowledge learning, practical learning, assessment and other functions. Based on the actual requirements of the site, the real digital twin model is constructed to realize the primary equipment operation simulation, secondary system operation simulation, operation simulation, safety measure arrangement simulation and maintenance scheme verification. On the field investigation and data collection, carry out theoretical analysis and model building method and process design, based on the operation and maintenance pain points. The system described in this paper constructs the functional structure of two plus five:

(1) Field environment cognition: build the field environment through the combination of lidar and field shooting, so as to help trainees to be familiar with the actual operating environment without going to the site.

(2) Cognitive function of single equipment: Through the construction of parts ledger, flexible view of the internal structure of the equipment can be realized, key parts can be displayed in isolation, key observation can be made, and other shielding parts can be hidden to realize the perspective of the equipment, as shown in Figure 1.

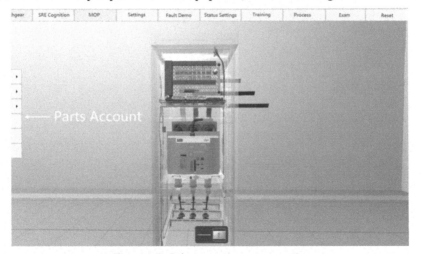

Figure 1. Switchroom equipment perspective

(3) Five anti-locking function: five anti-locking is an important guarantee for the safety of electrical operation, usually the meaning of the locking function can only be expressed in the form of text description due to safety reasons, abstract, difficult to understand the specific internal locking mode and principle. Through the training system of three-dimensional visual training system, the principle of mechanical and electrical locking can be truly restored, providing the opportunity for trial and error.

(4) Dangerous point display function: in reality, the electrical safety distance is often difficult to grasp, especially in the maintenance operations, the need to remove the permanent blocking, fence and other operations, it is very easy to exceed the safe distance. Through 3Dvisualization, high-voltage charged parts and safe distances can be displayed in a specific way in the 3Dspace, so as to provide a function of sensing dangerous points on the field in the virtual environment and establish danger sensitivity, thus reducing the risk of electric shock in the real world, as shown in Figure 2.

(5) Fault demonstration function: the lack of problems is an important way for power operation, maintenance and maintenance personnel to accumulate experience, only by accumulating a lot of experience can they avoid danger in the work, and such accidents are available but not available, so the training efficiency is often low, and the training cycle is long. All kinds of fault phenomena can be reproduced in the virtual 3Dspace, so as to help students quickly accumulate experience, get familiar with the causes of different faults, and the dangerous points generated in different fault situations.

Figure 2. Display of dangerous points

(6) Teaching function of safety rules: The traditional safety rules teaching is only taught through text or video methods, which is very abstract and boring. Although behind each provision is a lesson of blood and tears, it is difficult for students to form a deep impression. By constructing a standardized operation process in the three-dimensional space, carrying out safety procedures teaching in an intuitive and three-dimensional way, which can greatly deepen the impression of students, cultivate good operation and handling habits, and avoid habitual violations.

Assessment (7) the safety procedures: the traditional assessment can only be conducted by paper, but safety is involved in many field, so the best practice of safety regulations assessment should be field, but because the electrical equipment high voltage charged can not allow students wrong, in violation of safety norms, so it is difficult to carry out field assessment. However, in the virtual 3Dspace, the security risks are completely avoided, so the 3Ddigital assessment of all safety behaviors can be realized, which can not only record each step of operation, but also accurately score according to each behavior, greatly improving the assessment effect of safety procedures.

4. 3D visualization training system

Creating a switch room in the virtual space with the same properties as the real physical world can be considered to build the switch room in the metacoverse. The so-called attributes cover the appearance, size, mechanical attributes, electrical attributes, sound, light, operation logic and other aspects, the use of three-dimensional engine drive, so that the attributes of the digital virtual switch room in a variety of corresponding forms expressed. In this way, various kinds of simulation training can be carried out in the virtual digital space, such as operation state, fault state, operation simulation, five anti-lock simulation, etc. Compared with the current world, such simulation and simulation in digital space has many advantages: viewing devices from the perspective of God can greatly improve the cognitive efficiency of devices, three-dimensional view of complex institutions, extremely convenient component search, safe and risk-free operation, and so on.

For the above functions, the system described in this paper is developed based on U nity 3D 3Dengine, and constructs a 3Dvisualization training system that can truly restore the switch room site. The interface is shown in Figure 3.

Figure 3. System interface

In order to better realize the safety training function, the system not only built the switch room all related main equipment, including the incoming line cabinet, cabinet, pressure transformer cabinet, etc., also built a full set of safety instruments, including safety fence, red and white ribbon, warning signs, operation tools, insulation pad, etc., and according to the actual situation in the safety instrument box, as shown in Figure 4.

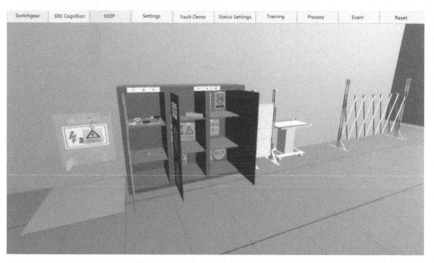

Figure 4. Safety tools and appliances

The above safety instruments can be placed freely in the scene. In the practice mode, the system can practice the layout of safety measures according to the requirements of the safety regulations. In the assessment mode, the wrong system will automatically judge and deduct points, as shown in Figure 5.

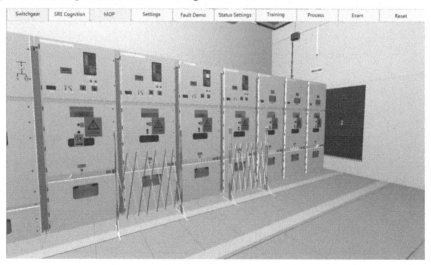

Figure 5. Arrangement of safety instruments

5. Conclusion

The interactive switch room safety procedure three-dimensional visualization training system is designed and developed. By building a digital three-dimensional scene with high reduction degree, the "simulated cockpit" of the power plant personnel is built, and the realization of the switch cabinet operation state, equipment operation, safety measures layout, work flow, training and assessment and other business simulation. In the "simulated cockpit", transport and maintenance personnel can operate freely, full trial and error, through a reasonable setting of feedback mechanism, can quickly improve personnel safety awareness and dangerous operation awareness. The successful development of this system can provide technical support for the innovative education mode of the safety regulations. The next step is to deepen the development of the digital assessment function, and realize the whole-process recording and evaluation of the operation behavior engineering.

References

[1] Qing Y, Shu-hua Z. Research review on development and evolution trend of virtual reality technology abroad. Dialectic of Nature Communication, 2021,43 (03): 97-106. doi:10.15994/j.1000-0763.2021.03.013.

[2] Ding-quan C, Jie S, Qing-yi W, Shiyu C, Wei-nan Z, Songlin P. Imagine the appearance of a library in the meta-universe between virtual and real. Library Forum, 2022,42 (01): 62-68.

[3] Zhi-qin C. Virtual reality industry development situation and response strategies. Technology Information, 2021,19 (24): 4-6. doi:10.16661/j.cnki.1672-3791.2109-5042-3857.

[4] Jian-ming L, Ming-tai S, Yu-lin Z, Qing-shan L. Application of augmented reality, virtual reality and mixed reality technologies in power systems. Electric Power Information and Communication Technology, 2017,15 (04): 4-11. doi:10.16543/j.2095-641x.electric.power.ict.2017.04.001.

[5] Xiao-ping Z, Zhi-liang H, Jun-gen Improvement and implementation of scene rendering method for virtual reality power training system. Electrotechnical technology,2023, (1): 68-71. doi: 0.19768/ j.cnki. dgjs.2023.01.018.

[6] Chen-meng X, Si-ming Z, Peng Y, Jian-li Z, Boyan J. Typical Application and Prospect of digital twin technology in power grid operation. High Voltage Technology, 2021,47 (05): 1564-1575. doi: 10.13336/ j.1003-6520.hve.20201838.

[7] An-nan X, Wei-xiang Z, Hong Z, Zhen-shan L, Yu-ping J. Research on electric fire safety training system based on virtual reality technology. Xin xi ji shui,2021, (6): 154-159. Doi: 10.13274/j. cnki.hdzj.2021.06.028.

[8] Fenghai H. A substation simulation system based on virtual reality technology. Electrotechnical technology,2022 (02): 96-98. doi: 10.19768/j.cnki.dgjs.2022.02.035.

Computer Systems and Communication Technology
W. Zheng (Ed.)
© 2024 The Authors.

doi:10.3233/ATDE240010

Underwater Image Enhancement Based on Multiscale Fusion

Shang Xinping[a,1] and Wang Yi[b]
[a]*Dongguan City University*
[b]*Dongguan City University*

Abstract. To improve the visibility and clarity of images in underwater environment, this paper proposes an underwater image enhancement method based on multi-scale fusion. Firstly, the white balance method is used to correct the color of the underwater image, and the original color of the underwater elements is restored as much as possible. Secondly, the dark channel prior algorithm is used to solve the underwater image blur problem. Then, the CLAHE algorithm is used to enhance the contrast of the image. Finally, using weight allocation or fusion rules, multi-scale information and multi-stage fusion of the image are used to generate the final enhanced underwater image. Quantitative image quality evaluation indexes PSNR, SSIM and UIQE are used to evaluate underwater image quality. The results show that the proposed method can effectively solve the problem of underwater image color deviation, make the color of the image more accurate and natural, improve the contrast and brightness of the underwater image, and have better visual effect and richer detail information.

Keywords. Multi-scale fusion, white balance, CLAHE

1. Introduction

Underwater image acquisition is subject to factors such as absorption, scattering, and fluctuations in water bodies, resulting in challenges in image visibility and detail. Improving the quality and visualization of underwater images is essential to achieve accurate target detection, target recognition and image analysis. To overcome the problems in the underwater environment, many researchers have proposed various underwater image enhancement methods.

Mishra et [1] al. has improved and applied CLAHE to underwater image enhancement, this method enhances the contrast of underwater images, but in some cases, the method may cause some details of the image to become blurred. Drews et al. [2] improved the classic dark channel prior (DCP) algorithm [3] combined with underwater characteristics and achieved remarkable results in underwater image denoising and fog removal, but it did not get sufficient improvement for the common color distortion problem in underwater images. Zhang Wei et al. [4] proposed low-illumination underwater image enhancement based on white balance and relative total variational, which improved the color performance of underwater images and further improved the image quality. However, underwater images still face serious problems of atomization and low contrast. In recent years, deep learning methods can generally obtain clear

---

[1] Corresponding Author: Shang Xinping, 66629426@qq.com.

underwater images. Li et [5] al used generative adversarial network to correct the color bias problem, Wang Haotian et [6] al proposed cyclic generative adversarial network to correct the color, and Xu Yan et[7] al used convolutional neural network to improve the image quality based on the underwater image imaging model. All these methods have made remarkable progress in underwater image processing. However, these methods usually require a large amount of paired training data, which is very difficult and expensive to obtain, limiting the universality and application of deep learning methods.

Ancuti et [8] al. is an effective method for multi-scale fusion of images that have been processed in different ways, which can produce better processing results. The research in this paper and other fusion strategies can effectively improve the quality of underwater images, to improve the observation effect of images more comprehensively and provide a better foundation for underwater image processing and related applications.

2. Underwater image enhancement algorithm

Due to the special nature of underwater optical imaging, the acquired images generally have problems such as color distortion, low contrast, and blurred details. To solve these problems, the underwater image processing flow designed in this paper is shown in Figure 1.

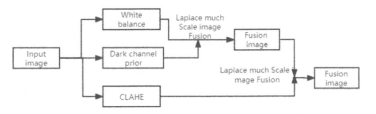

Figure 1. underwater image processing flow

Firstly, using the white balance algorithm to process the image can improve the visual effect of the underwater image, restore the image color, and adjust the color bias, eliminate the image noise and retain the image details; Secondly, the dark channel prior algorithm is used to solve the problem that the underwater image appears fuzzy due to a large number of suspended particles. Then, using CLAHE algorithm to effectively suppress the noise amplification and enhance the local contrast of the image, can improve the clarity and color brightness of the image, and has a good effect on the image atomization phenomenon; Finally, according to the weight allocation or fusion rules, Laplacian multi-scale image fusion is used in multiple stages to generate the final enhanced image. The principle of each step is described in detail next.

2.1. White Balance algorithm

Adaptive white balance is an algorithm used to correct the color of an image, aiming to eliminate color bias problems in the image. Its principle is based on the color perception features of the human eye. The human eye has a strong perception of light color temperature and can automatically adjust the color deviation in visual perception according to the light conditions in the environment, so that the colors seen remain consistent. Specifically, the algorithm will adjust the color value of each pixel in the image according to the perceived light color temperature information by increasing or reducing the color value of the three channels of red, green and blue in each pixel. In this way, the white object in the image can show the true white under different light conditions, and other colors can also maintain relatively accurate colors. Fig. 2 Results of adaptive white balance. (a) Original image; (b) processing results of gray world algorithm; (c) processing results of adaptive white balance, the proposed method corrects the color distortion of underwater images and effectively removes the color bias of green, blue and yellow.

image1   Image2   Image3
(a)   (b)   (c)   (a)   (b)   (c)   (a)   (b)   (c)

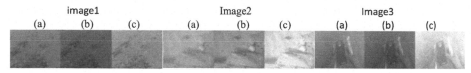

Figure 2. Results of adaptive white balance

2.2. Dark channel prior

Dark channel prior aims to remove fog and improve image clarity and contrast by analyzing dark channel features in images. Its principle can be briefly summarized as follows: First, calculate the dark channel, for the input image, calculate the minimum value of each pixel on different channels, and assign to the corresponding pixel in the dark channel image, recompose the grayscale image, and then carry on the minimum filtering to the image to obtain the dark channel image. Secondly, according to the dark channel image, select the area with higher brightness in the image, and estimate the atmospheric light intensity. Finally, using the estimated atmospheric light intensity, the original image is de-fogged and enhanced. FIG. 3 Results of dark channel prior. (a) The original image; And (b) the result of the dark channel prior algorithm.

(a)   (b)

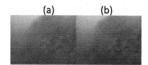

Figure 3. Results of dark channel prior

2.3. CLAHE

CLAHE is an algorithm for image enhancement, full name Contrast Limod Adaptvo Hislogram Equalizatlon, its principle is summarized as follows: First, the image is divided into many small pieces, each of which is the size of NxN; Secondly, histogram equalization is performed on each small block, so that the distribution of pixel values in each small block is more even; Then, the equalized image cable is restricted to avoid excessive enhancement. Finally, all the small pieces are stitched together to get the enhanced image. This algorithm can enhance the contrast of the image and make the details clearer by equalizing and limiting the image with local hundred squares. FIG. 4 Results of CLAHE algorithm. (a) The original image; And (b) the results of CLAHE's algorithm.

(a)   (b)

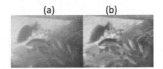

Figure 4. Results of CLAHE algorithm

3. Experimental results and analysis

The hardware system of the experiment is Intel Core i5-12500H, and the memory is 16GB; The software environment is Python and Win11 operating system. In order to verify the feasibility of this method, multiple images with different degradation characteristics were selected from the underwater image dataset UIEB[9] , as shown in FIG. 5 (a). The first, second and third images showed obvious green, blue or yellow color deviation with low clarity, while the fourth, fifth and sixth images showed obvious insufficient illumination and low visibility. The algorithm in this paper is compared with other algorithms, and the experimental results of different algorithms are analyzed from both subjective and objective aspects.

3.1. Subjective evaluation

In this paper, 6 kinds of images under different underwater environments are selected for comparison experiment, and the processing results are shown in Figure 5. As can be seen from FIG. 5 (e), the algorithm in this paper can solve the problem of color decay in different underwater environments on the whole on the premise of avoiding excessive enhancement. The contrast is greatly improved, and the local details of the image are clear and obvious, which accords with the image under natural light.

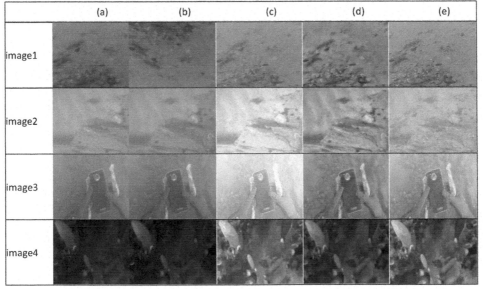

Figure 5. Results of six different image enhancement algorithms

3.2. Objective evaluation

This paper uses three performance indicators to evaluate underwater image quality, namely PSNR, SSIM and UIQE[10] . PSNR is based on the error calculation between corresponding pixel points, mainly calculating the ratio between the maximum signal and the background noise. The larger the value, the smaller the distortion. The calculation formula is as follows:

$$MSE = \frac{1}{H*W}\sum_{i=1}^{H}\sum_{j=1}^{W}[X(i,j) - Y(i,j)]^2 \tag{1}$$

$$PSNR = 10\log_{10}\left(\frac{(2^n-1)^2}{MSE}\right) \tag{2}$$

Where: MSE represents the mean square error of the image; H and W represent the width and height of the image; n represents the number of bits of the image pixel. SSIM is a measure of the similarity of two images and is calculated by the formula.

$$SSIM = \frac{(2x_1x_2+C_1)(2y_{1,2}+C_2)}{(x_1^2+x_2^2+C_1)(y_1^2+y_2^2+C_2)} \tag{3}$$

Where: x_1, y_1 represents the mean value and standard deviation of the input image; $y_1 \setminus y_2$ represents the mean value and standard deviation of the enhanced image; $y_{1,2}$ Represents the covariance of the input image and the enhanced image; C_1, C_2 is a constant. The larger the SSIM value, the smaller the structural loss of the input original. UIQE is a special index used to evaluate the quality of underwater images. Usually, different weight parameters are fine-tuned for the three components of color fidelity, contrast and sharpness according to the underwater environment. The determination of the three weight parameters needs to be calculated by multivariate linear regression, and finally the final index is obtained by linear addition of different components.

$$UIQE = C_1 * \alpha + C_2 * \beta + C_3 * \gamma \tag{4}$$

Where: C_1, C_2, C_3 are the weights of different components; α Represents the measurement index of color fidelity; β Represents the contrast measurement index; γ Represents a measure of clarity. The objective evaluation data of the above experiments are shown in Table 1. It can be seen from Table 1 that the values of the three evaluation indexes of the algorithm in this paper are almost optimal. Objectively, it shows that the algorithm in this paper retains more original image information. Among them, the larger the UIQE value, the better the color fidelity, clarity, and contrast of the image.

Table 1. Objective quality assessment of Figure 5

Metric	method	image1	image 2	image 3	Image4	image5	image6
PSNR	WB	12.6239	9.1141	6.3107	12.4238	15.8898	8.7089
	DCP	25.1648	22.4377	27.4336	41.5086	21.2399	23.9710
	CLAHE	21.4773	22.0480	23.9710	22.0350	21.4857	20.256
	OURS	26.4460	22.3580	28.2080	42.0512	25.1876	24.0019
SSIM	WB	0.7034	0.7431	0.5770	0.3700	0.3700	0.4329
	DCP	0.8649	0.8466	0.8704	0.9484	0.9484	0.8745
	CLAHE	0.7873	0.8048	0.8447	0.7045	0.7045	0.7591
	OURS	0.8207	0.8038	0.8892	0.9722	0.8722	0.8911
UIQE	WB	0.4522	0.2296	0.36164	0.76715	0.3383	0.3530
	DCP	0.5810	0.33513	0.42771	0.2345	0.1233	0.4723
	CLAHE	0.3017	0.3409	0.5129	0.6235	0.3707	0.5538
	OURS	0.6537	0.3559	0.5467	0.6613	0.5121	0.6305

4. Conclusion

This study proposes an underwater image enhancement method based on multi-scale fusion, aiming to improve the visibility and clarity of images in underwater environments. Through a combination of steps such as white balance, dark channel prior, CLAHE algorithm processing and multi-stage and multi-scale fusion for underwater images, underwater noise and interference components can be more comprehensively suppressed, and useful image details and structures can be highlighted. The experimental results verify the effectiveness of the image enhancement method, which makes the color of the image more accurate and natural, improves the contrast and brightness of the underwater image, and has better visual effect and richer detail information.

References

[1] Mishra A, Gupta M, Sharma P. Enhancement of underwater images using improved CLAHE [C]//2018 International Conference on Advanced Computing and Telecommunications (ICACAT), 2018:1-6
[2] Drews P L, Nascimento E R, Botelho S S, et al. Underwater depth estimation and image restoration based on single images [J] IEEE Computer Graphics and Applications 2016,36 (2): 24-35
[3] He K M, Sun J, Tang X. Single Image Haze Removal Using Dark Channel Prior [C]//2009 IEEE Conference on Computer Vision and Pattern Recognition, June 20-25, 2009, Miami, Florida, USA. New York: IEEE, 2009
[4] ZHANG W, GUO J C. Low illumination underwater image enhancement based on white balance and relative total variation [J] Advances in Laser and Optoelectronics, 2020, 57 (12): 213-220
[5] Chongyi L, Chunle G, Wenqi R, et al. An Underwater Image Enhancement Benchmark Dataset and Beyond [J] . IEEE transactions on image processing: a publication of the IEEE Signal Processing Society, 2019,29
[6] Wang Haotian, Liu Qingsheng, Chen Liang, et al. Improved CycleGAN network for color correction of underwater microscopic images [J]. Optical Precision Engineering, 2022,30 (12): 1499-1508
[7] Xu Yan, Sun Meishuang. Underwater Image Enhancement Method Based on Convolutional Neural Networks [J]. Journal of Jilin University (Engineering Edition), 2018,48 (06): 1895-1903. doi: 10.13229/j.cnki.jdxbgxb20170815
[8] Cosmin A, Codruta O A, Tom H, et al Enhancing under underwater images and video by fusion [C], IEEE Conference on Computer Vision and Pattern Recognition, 2012:81-88
[9] Chongyi L, Chunle G, Wenqi R, et al. An Underwater Image Enhancement Benchmark Dataset and Beyond [J]. Journal of Technology, 2020, 29: 4376-438
[10] Miao Y, Arcot S. An Underwater Color Image Quality Evaluation Metric [J] . IEEE transactions on image processing: a publication of the IEEE Signal Processing Society, 2015,24 (12)

Computer Systems and Communication Technology
W. Zheng (Ed.)
© 2024 The Authors.
This article is published online with Open Access by IOS Press and distributed under the terms
of the Creative Commons Attribution Non-Commercial License 4.0 (CC BY-NC 4.0).
doi:10.3233/ATDE240011

Semiconductor Material Porosity Segmentation in Flame Retardant Materials SEM Images Using Data Augmentation and Transfer Learning

Siwei Lu[a], Xiaofang Zhao[b1], Huazhu Liu[b], Hongjie Liang[b]

[a]*College of Electronic and Information Engineering, Shenzhen University, ShenzhenCity, China;*
[b]*International School of Microelectronics, Dongguan University of Technology, DongguanCity, China*

Abstract. Non-halogenated flame retardants are becoming the trend in the development of polymer flame retardant materials due to their high flame retardant efficiency and low generation of toxic smoke gases. Non-halogenated flame retardants achieve flame retardancy by forming a dense char layer and generating non-combustible gases, with the micro-porous structure of the char residue being crucial for studying the flame retardant mechanism. This study focuses on the segmentation of pores in scanning electron microscopy (SEM) images of the combustion char layer of non-halogenated flame retardant materials, which are cropped and labeled to form a unified dataset. We investigate the SEM image pore segmentation using data augmentation and transfer learning, addressing the challenge of limited sample size. We explore the impact of different data augmentation techniques and transfer learning on model performance. Additionally, we compare convolutional neural network (CNN) segmentation algorithms with traditional segmentation methods. Experimental results demonstrate that CNN segmentation algorithms outperform traditional methods in terms of segmentation accuracy. Offline data augmentation enhances model stability compared to online data augmentation, and adopting transfer learning significantly improves model performance metrics. Specifically, when training with VGG backbone weights through transfer learning, the average pixel accuracy and average intersection over union reach 94.49% and 89.88%, respectively.

Keywords. SEM Image Segmentation, Non-halogenated flame retardant materials, data augmentation, transfer learning

1. Introduction

With the continuous advancement of science and technology, an increasing number of polymer materials are being integrated into our daily lives. However, most polymer products possess the drawback of being highly flammable. Therefore, the development of flame-retardant polymer materials has become a prominent focus in various industries. Based on the composition of flame retardants, polymer materials can be categorized into

---

[1] Corresponding Author:Xiaofang Zhao, zhaoxf@dgut.edu.cn

two main types: those containing halogen-based flame retardants and those containing halogen-free flame retardants. In contrast, halogen-free flame retardants are highly efficient in retarding combustion and produce fewer toxic smoke gases. Consequently, they have gained widespread acceptance and application in various polymer products[1-2]. Among these halogen-free flame retardants, ammonium polyphosphate and pentaerythritol are representative examples. These flame-retardant actions are primarily achieved through two mechanisms. First, they catalyze the formation of a dense char layer, effectively blocking the transfer of oxygen, flammable gases, and heat. Second, they undergo thermal decomposition to generate non-flammable gases. Of particular importance in understanding the condensed-phase flame-retardant mechanism is the microstructure of the resulting char layer, with a focus on its microscopic pores[1-3].Among various methods for studying the microstructure of char residues, scanning electron microscopy (SEM) has emerged as the predominant technique[4].In the context of SEM pore images of shale, Wang et al. [5] and others manually selected appropriate threshold segmentation methods, effectively segmenting shale pores above 1nm, and conducted quantitative analysis of shale pore structures. Chen et al. [6] designed a deep fully convolutional neural network called FLU-net based on pixel-level semantic segmentation to classify shale pores into organic pores, inorganic pores, and fractures. This paragraph is intended for publication at an international conference and has been translated into English using professional terminology.

Currently, deep learning has made significant breakthroughs in fields such as medical image segmentation, image recognition, natural language processing, and more. The concept of Few-shot Learning[7,8]has been introduced to address the fundamental problem of learning from a limited number of examples. Few-shot learning comes in three primary forms: model fine-tuning, data augmentation, and transfer learning[9]. The core challenge in few-shot learning lies in the scarcity of effective samples, which leads to reduced sample diversity. Therefore, in situations where data is limited, improving sample diversity through Data Augmentation[10]can enhance a model's ability to extract features effectively. Transfer learning[11] involves transferring knowledge learned from a source domain to a target domain.

This paper combines data augmentation and transfer learning and applies them to the domain of SEM image segmentation of halogen-free flame-retardant thermoplastic polyurethane materials. Through comparative experiments, it investigates the differences between deep learning segmentation methods and traditional segmentation methods. Additionally, it explores the impact of various data augmentation techniques and transfer learning training strategies on model performance. This study provides valuable insights into the intelligent evaluation of flame-retardant properties in halogen-free flame-retardant materials.

2. Materials and methods

2.1. Data Preprocessing

Since there is currently no publicly available dataset of SEM images of flame-retardant materials after combustion, this study prepared a dataset by using the melt-blending method. Two flame retardants, ammonium polyphosphate (APP) and pentaerythritol (PER), were added to thermoplastic polyurethane elastomer (TPU) in different proportions to create a series of flame-retardant TPU composites. These composites were then incinerated to form a series of char residues. Microscopic images of these char residues were obtained using scanning electron microscopy (SEM) to establish the dataset.

From a total of 1184 SEM images of the char residues captured, 117 images containing well-defined pore structures and good quality were selected. These images were resized to a uniform dimension of 1280×760 and annotated using the labelme tool. An example of a flame-retardant material SEM image is shown in Figure 1(a), and the annotated version is presented in Figure 1(b), where the red regions represent pore areas, and the black regions represent background areas. Figure 2 provides examples of SEM images from the flame-retardant material dataset, illustrating variations in pore quantity and distribution among different images.

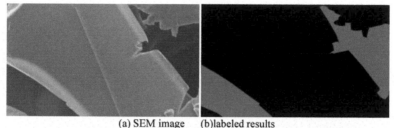

(a) SEM image   (b)labeled results

Figure1. Flame-retardant material SEM image sample and its labeling results

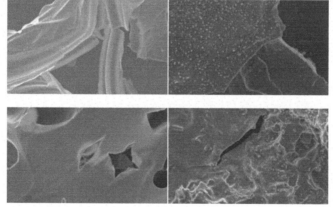

Figure 2. Selected Image Samples

2.2. Data Augmentation

To address the issue of limited data, data augmentation is commonly employed. Its primary objective is to generate a more diverse dataset by applying deterministic transformations to the existing data, thereby mitigating the risk of model overfitting, enhancing generalization performance, and improving the model's resistance to interference. Data augmentation can be categorized into two types: online data augmentation, where various transformations are applied to images during training to increase dataset diversity, and offline data augmentation, where the dataset is expanded through transformations before training to reduce redundant computations during data import.

In this study, both types of augmentation were utilized during model training, although the specific transformation operations were the same. The data augmentation methods included resizing, rotation, scaling, flipping, sharpening, and blurring, as illustrated in Figure 3. For online augmentation, 100 iterations were applied, effectively increasing the dataset by a factor of 100, with each image being used for training once. For offline augmentation, the dataset was expanded by a factor of 10 through transformations, with 10 iterations for each image during training.

2.3. Research methods in this paper

In this study, the deep convolutional neural network employs a two-part algorithm: the visual geometry group (VGG)[12] network model with the fully connected layers removed and the encoder part of the UNet network[13], both consisting of stacked convolutional layers. The initial training is performed on the first part using transfer learning from the VGG network. Subsequently, the UNet network's decoder is employed to restore the original image dimensions and make segmentation predictions. For small-sample annotated data, we leverage pre-training on existing large-scale datasets and employ transfer learning to migrate feature extraction parameters to the new network. This approach enhances the model's generalization capabilities and reduces its dependency on the training dataset.

3. Experiments and resulte

3.1. Evaluation Metrics

In order to quantitatively assess the performance of the experimental models, this study employs the following segmentation accuracy evaluation metrics: Mean Pixel Accuracy (MPA) measures the percentage of correctly predicted pixels over the total number of pixels in all images. Mean Intersection over Union (MIoU) calculates the intersection over union for each image and then computes the mean value. It quantifies the overlap between predicted and ground truth masks. Precision represents the ratio of true positive predictions to the total positive predictions, measuring the accuracy of positive predictions. Recall, also known as sensitivity or true positive rate, assesses the proportion of true positive predictions to the actual positives in the ground truth. F1 Score is the harmonic mean of precision and recall, providing a balance between these two metrics.

3.2. Training Process

After splitting the training samples into groups, the model is cross-trained and tested, aiming to produce segmentation results that closely resemble the ground truth. During the training of the pre-trained deep transfer learning model, freezing and unfreezing operations are performed. The purpose of these operations is to prevent the training of the new model from disturbing the learned features of the pre-training phase and to adapt the model's parameters to the new dataset. This approach helps ensure that the model effectively leverages the knowledge learned during pre-training while fine-tuning it for improved performance on the new dataset.

3.3. Comparative Experiments

In order to investigate the impact of data augmentation methods and transfer learning training strategies on model performance, the following ablation experiments were designed: Experiment1: Training set uses online data augmentation without using transfer learning. Experiment 2: Training set uses offline data augmentation without using transfer learning. Experiment 3: Training set uses online data augmentation with pre-training by loading VGG backbone network weights. Experiment 4: Training set uses offline data augmentation with pre-training by loading VGG backbone network weights. In these experiments, the VGG backbone network weights are initialized using pre-trained weights obtained from a large-scale dataset like ImageNet before training. The training loss variations during the experimental training process are depicted in Figure 3. It is evident that all four experiments exhibit loss convergence. Experiments employing transfer learning demonstrate faster convergence compared to those without direct training. The weights corresponding to the epochs with the best overall training performance were selected for each experiment, and testing was conducted on the test dataset, as presented in Table 1.

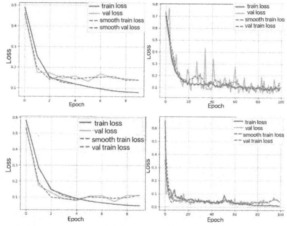

Figure 3. Changes in experimental losses

Table 1. Effects of data enhancement and migration learning on experimental results

	MIoU	MPA	Precision	Recall	F1
Exp1	85.20%	87.62%	96.35%	87.62%	91.78%
Exp2	77.47%	87.88%	84.54%	87.88%	86.18%
Exp3	87.68%	96.60%	90.14%	96.60%	93.26%
Exp4	89.88%	94.49%	94.43%	94.48%	94.46%

3.4. Comparative Results Analysis

Comparing the results of Experiments 1 and 3, which both employed online data augmentation without transfer learning, the MIoU was 85.20% for Experiment 1 and 87.68% for Experiment 3, showing an improvement of 2.48% when VGG backbone weights were transferred. Contrasting the outcomes of Experiments 2 and 4, where offline data augmentation was applied without transfer learning, Experiment 2 achieved an MIoU of 77.47%, while Experiment 4, with VGG backbone weight transfer, reached an MIoU of 89.88%, marking an increase of 12.41%. Transfer learning significantly enhanced the model training results, with the highest MIoU achieved being 89.88% when using offline data augmentation and backbone transfer.

Comparing Experiments 1 and 2, as well as Experiments 3 and 4, where the network architecture remained unchanged, the focus was solely on contrasting online and offline data augmentation. When not utilizing transfer learning, the average intersection over union (IoU) was higher for online data augmentation compared to offline data augmentation. Online data augmentation dynamically generates transformed samples for each training batch, with each batch's samples being independently generated. This dynamic variation exposes the model to a broader and richer range of data changes, thereby enhancing the model's generalization capability and adaptability.In contrast, when transfer learning was applied, the average IoU was higher for offline data augmentation compared to online data augmentation. Offline data augmentation preprocesses the data before training, incorporating the generated augmented data alongside the original data for training. This approach allows for more controlled and targeted introduction of additional sample variations and diversity during the training process. The F1 score for offline data augmentation was overall higher than that for online data augmentation, indicating that training the network with offline data augmentation is more stable.

It's important to note that transfer learning improved the model's convergence speed. Thus, in this study, transfer learning not only significantly enhanced training performance but also notably reduced training time. In conclusion, Experiment 4, utilizing offline data augmentation and VGG backbone weight transfer, yielded the best overall training performance. Compared to the model without transfer learning, this approach achieved superior segmentation results and greater stability.

3.5. Comparison Between the Proposed Algorithm and Traditional Segmentation Methods

Traditional SEM image segmentation methods include region growing, threshold-based segmentation, and watershed segmentation algorithms. In this section, we compare the segmentation performance of the training approach with the highest MPA in our study, which utilizes offline data augmentation and VGG backbone weight transfer, against the segmentation accuracy achieved by the three aforementioned algorithms. Figure 4 displays the comparative results of the four algorithms.

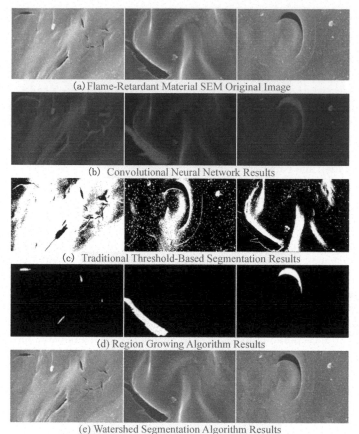

(a) Flame-Retardant Material SEM Original Image

(b) Convolutional Neural Network Results

(c) Traditional Threshold-Based Segmentation Results

(d) Region Growing Algorithm Results

(e) Watershed Segmentation Algorithm Results

Figure 4. Comparison Between Convolutional Neural Network Algorithm and Traditional Segmentation Algorithms

From Figure 4, several observations can be made:Traditional threshold segmentation algorithms are ineffective in extracting pores due to the presence of local highlights and uneven grayscale distribution in SEM images.The region growing algorithm performs better compared to traditional threshold segmentation, but it requires manual selection of seed points. This process is cumbersome, and the choice of seed point locations is random and relies on operator judgment, resulting in poor reproducibility and less-than-ideal pore edge segmentation.

The watershed segmentation algorithm (marked by the blue line) identifies pore areas but tends to over-segment due to the presence of many local minima in the grayscale distribution, leading to excessive splitting.

In contrast, our approach, based on a fully convolutional network, achieves SEM image pore segmentation without the need for manual seed point selection. It effectively segments pore regions and ensures the complete segmentation of fine pores. The segmentation accuracy is significantly higher than that of traditional segmentation methods.

4. Conclusion

In this study, we integrated data augmentation with transfer learning and applied them to the field of SEM image pore segmentation in flame-retardant materials. We constructed an SEM dataset of flame-retardant materials based on electron scanning microscopy images of non-halogen flame-retardant thermoplastic polyurethane combustion residue layers. Through comparative experiments, we investigated the impact of data augmentation techniques and transfer learning strategies on model performance. Additionally, we compared deep learning segmentation methods with traditional segmentation approaches. The experimental results demonstrate that, compared to traditional segmentation algorithms, deep learning algorithms yield more accurate segmentation results. Furthermore, utilizing transfer learning training strategies enhances segmentation accuracy. Offline data augmentation methods also result in improved model stability compared to online data augmentation techniques. Accurate segmentation of SEM image pores, coupled with pore density, pore shape, size, and distribution, enables automatic classification of flame-retardant material fire resistance levels.

References

[1] Yang Q Q, Xu S L, Qiang F Z, et al. Study on fractal dimension of SEM images of solid propellant[J]. Chem. Propellants Polymer. Mater, 2021, 19: 63-67.doi:10.16572/j.issn1672-2191.202109010

[2] Song H, Min L, Jun X, et al. Fractal characteristic of three Chinese coals[J]. Fuel, 2004, 83(10): 1307-1313.doi:10.1016/j.fuel.2003.12.011

[3] Xue Meigui, Chen Hongqian, Li Hui, et al. Calculation of Porosity of Printing Paper Based on Threshold Regression Method Using SEM Images. China Pulp & Paper, 2020, 39(05): 50-54. doi:10.11980/j.issn.0254-508X.2020.05.008.

[4] Zheng Xin, You Jichun, Zhu Yutian, Li Yongjin. Application of Scanning Electron Microscopy in Polymer Characterization Research. Acta PolymericaSinica, 2022, 53(05): 539-560. doi:10.11777/j.issn1000-3304.2021.21377

[5] Wang Yu, Jin Chan, Wang Lihua, Wang Jianqiang, Jiang Zheng, Wang Yanfei. Research on Shale Pore Segmentation Method Based on SEM Image Gray Level[J]. Rock and Mineral Analysis, 2016, 35(06): 595-602.doi: 10.15898/j.cnki.11-2131/td.2016.06.005

[6] Chen Yan, Li Zhicheng, Cheng Chao, Jiao Shixiang, Jiang Yuqiang, Song Min, Wang Zhanlei. FLU-net: A Deep Fully Convolutional Network for Characterizing Microscopic Pores in Shale Reservoirs[J]. Frontiers of Marine Geology, 2021, 37(08): 34-43.doi: 10.16028/j.1009-2722.2019.196

[7] Jankowski N, Duch W, Grąbczewski K. Meta-learning in Computational Intelligence[J].. Springer Science and Business Media, 2011. 97-115.doi: 10.1007/978-3-642-20980-2

[8] Mahbub U , Imtiaz H , Roy T ,et al.A template matching approach of one-shot-learning gesture recognition[J].Pattern Recognition Letters, 2013, 34(15):1780-1788.DOI:10.1016/j.patrec.2012.09.014.

[9] Zhao Kailin, Jin Xiaolong, Wang Yuanzhuo. A Survey of Few-shot Learning Research. Journal of Software, 2021, 32(02): 349-369.doi: 10.13328/j.cnki.jos.006138

[10] Royle JA, Dorazio RM, Link WA. Analysis of multinomial models with unknown index using data augmentation[J].. Journal of Computational and Graphical Statistics, 2007,16(1):67−85.doi: 10.1198/106186007X181425

[11] Liu XP, Luan XD, Xie YX, et al. Transfer learning research and algorithm review[J].. Journal of Changsha University, 2018,32(5): 33−36,41 . doi:10.3969/j.issn.1008-4681.2018.05.008

[12] Ronneberger O, Fischer P, Brox T. U-net: Convolutional networks for biomedical image segmentation[C]//Medical Image Computing and Computer-Assisted Intervention–MICCAI 2015: 18th International Conference, Munich, Germany, October 5-9, 2015, Proceedings, Part III 18. Springer International Publishing, 2015: 234-241.doi: 10.1007/978-3-319-24574-4_28

[13] Simonyan, Karen, and Andrew Zisserman. "Very deep convolutional networks for large-scale image recognition." arXiv preprint arXiv:1409.1556 (2014).doi: 10.48550/arXiv.1409.1556

Computer Systems and Communication Technology
W. Zheng (Ed.)

Subject Index

Computer Systems and Communication Technology
W. Zheng (Ed.)
© *2024 The Authors.*

85

Author Index